A View from the Firehouse:
The Newark Riots

Additional books by author:

Firehouse Fraternity Oral History Series:
Volume I: Becoming a Firefighter
Volume II: Life Between Alarms
Volume III: Equipment
Volume IV: Responding
Volume V: Riots to Renaissance
Volume VI: Changing the NFD

An Eerie Silence: An Oral History of Newark
Firefighters at the WTC

Hervey's Boys: New Jersey's First Chinese Community
1870-1886 (And What Happened After That)

Fiction:
The Firebox Stalker
The Hand Life Dealt you
A-zou: A Woman Living in Interesting Times

Children's Fiction:
A Hundred Battles (YA)
A Broken Glass (YA)
Balancing Act (Middle Grade)

A View from the Firehouse: The Newark Riots

Neal Stoffers

Springfield and Hunterdon Publishing
Copyright 2006
www.newarkfireoralhistory.com

First Printing: 2006

ISBN 978-1-970034-03-5

Springfield and Hunterdon Publishing
East Brunswick, NJ 08816

Dedicated to Captain Michael "Mike" Moran
Killed in the Line of Duty
July 15, 1967

Acknowledgements

The credit for much of this book goes to the members of the Newark Fire Department who gave so generously of their time to take part in my oral history project. The hours of recorded conversations they contributed will help preserve the history of Newark's fire department and of Newark itself. A list of those interviewed appears after the narrative. This is their story. I am honored to tell it.

Foreword

As a young Newark firefighter, I walked into the quarters of Six Engine on Springfield Avenue and Hunterdon Street in January 1979. I had just been assigned to the company. For the most part, the men who greeted me were too young to remember what had happened along Springfield Avenue eleven and a half years before. The only exceptions were the Deputy Chief, his driver, and the senior man assigned to the Engine. The last three would provide me with my introduction to the experiences of the fire department during the riots.

Besides the stories passed on to the next generation of firefighters, there were the casual remarks while working in front of the firehouse. As we washed the apparatus, bullet holes in the side of the building next door and chips in the firehouse bricks caused by shots fired from the projects that towered over the area were pointed out. These sights and stories became part of being a member of this company. The quiet matter of fact manner of their telling only added to the respect felt for the men speaking. Occasionally, we would take out the company journal from that July and read the entries. All the time realizing that few people outside the fire department could imagine what these men had gone through. It is my hope this short book will shed some light on these experiences so a changing world will not forget what was sacrificed.

The material in this book was originally prepared for a conference sponsored by the New Jersey Historical Society and the Rutgers University Institute on Ethnicity, Culture, and the Modern Experience. Entitled *1960s Conflicts in Context: Race, Ethnicity, and Urban Unrest in Post War New Jersey,* this conference took place in November 2004.

Very little has been published on the fire department's role during the July, 1967 civil disturbance in Newark. The paper submitted to this conference was an attempt to correct this omission. I have been compiling an oral history of the Newark Fire Department since June of 1991 and so was able to tap the memories of NFD personnel who had contributed to this project. This is their story often told in their own words. The view of the 1967 riots told here is not the view seen from City Hall, Trenton, or the hearing rooms of Congress. The view presented here is on ground level. It is simply the view from the firehouse.

Prologue

The civil disturbance of 1967 was a watershed in the history of Newark. Known simply as "the riots" to a generation of Newarkers; the melee that July altered life in New Jersey's largest city in ways that are still felt today. It was a defining moment for the city's fire department. Newark firefighters emerged from the four nights of mayhem forever changed. From the experiences of the department during those July nights, they developed and used strategies and tactics that had never seriously been considered before.

Newark in 1967 was a city on the edge. Watts had exploded in August 1965. Chicago had similar problems the following summer. The spring of 1967 saw troubles at three southern colleges, as well as, Tampa, Cincinnati, and Atlanta. Racial tensions in Newark had gone from bad to worse during this time. Issues and disagreements continued to mount as summer approached. Mayor Hugh Addonizio lobbied extensively for the New Jersey College of Medicine and Dentistry to be built in the Central Ward. The area proposed for the hospital's location was home for hundreds of African-American families living in dilapidated buildings. After several meetings with the Mayor, the African community perceived his administration as heavy handed and unresponsive to its needs. A violent confrontation on the Newark-East Orange border at the beginning of July only worsened the situation. To the men manning her firehouses, the city seemed ready to ignite.

At the time the city was protected by twenty-five engine (pumper) companies, twelve truck (ladder) companies, two salvage companies, a rescue squad, and a

1

fireboat. These units were divided into two deputy divisions which were subdivided into five battalion districts. The Central Ward, where tensions were highest, was in the First Deputy Division and for the most part in the Fourth Battalion district.[1]

The neighborhoods that surrounded the firehouses on Springfield Avenue, Belmont Avenue, Sherman Avenue, and Avon Avenue in the Central Ward had become increasingly hostile. An escalation of confrontations with angry citizens had begun around 1965. By 1967 harassment had become a part of the environment and fire crews tried to stay together. "We made sure there were at least four firemen always together. Nobody wandered off."[2] This was a dramatic change from past relations between the firefighters and the people they served. Only a few years before, firefighters had passed time between alarms sitting in front of the firehouse talking with the neighbors as they walked by. Citizens would "cut through our alley, open the back kitchen door; walk through the kitchen with us sitting there. Say hello. We'd say hello back, and they'd walk through the apparatus floor and go out the door."[3]

The change was a culmination of shifts in society that had begun after World War II. A large percentage of the housing stock in Newark was three-story frame tenements built at the turn of the century. Over 400,000 residents occupied these aging structures. Returning veterans found it hard to find housing in the city. If a

---

[1] Newark Fire Department Annual Report 1967. The Salvage units were responsible for minimizing water damage to fire buildings and for securing the building when the fire department left.
[2] Deputy Chief Ed Dunn, interview by author, 29 August 1997, transcript. (Hereafter Dunn)
[3] Deputy Chief Alfred Freda, interview by author, 12 July 1991, transcript. (Hereafter Freda)

2

house was found, it was difficult for a young couple to obtain a mortgage because the age of the building required a higher down payment. Veterans began to move to the burgeoning suburbs springing up along the newly completed New Jersey Turnpike and Garden State Parkway. By 1960, Newark's population had begun to contract.[4] Those left behind and the newly arriving residents were poorer and minorities. By 1967 the city's population had changed from one dominated by whites to one that was sixty-two percent minority, fifty-two percent of whom were African-Americans.[5] Their relations with the predominantly white Newark Police Department were strained.

Even if the men in a particular firehouse had a good rapport with their neighbors, people who lived away from the firehouses did not always appreciate firemen; who represented authority in the eyes of the disaffected. This change in sentiment was obvious to the firefighters. After the summer of 1965, the apprehension felt by fire companies when they responded to alarms was heightened. To the men responding to fire boxes, an indication that a breakdown was occurring in Newark's social fabric was the false alarm rate, which had been declining steadily since 1963. There were eight hundred seventy-four false alarms in 1965. The monthly rate was in double digits for eleven months of 1966, totaling nine hundred eighty-one for the year. January and February of 1967 each had sixty-nine malicious false alarms or "Signal 300's." In the months before the riots "it went

---

[4]Newark's population was recorded at 429,760 in 1940, 438,766 in 1950, and 405,000 in 1960.
[5]National Advisory Commission on Civil Disorders. *Report of the National Advisory Commission on Civil Disorders.* (Washington, D.C.: Government Printing Office, 1968; reprint, New York: Bantam Books, 1968), p. 57. (Hereafter National Commission)

off the end,"[6] climbing to one hundred sixty-nine the month before the explosion in July.[7]

In anticipation of possible trouble, the Planning Division of the Department had put together a blueprint for responding during civil disorders based on the experiences of the Los Angles Fire Department. The plan called for fire companies to leave their firehouses and assemble in staging areas from where they would be dispatched to fires as they were reported. This system rotated companies, so fire crews would be able to rest before responding to another alarm. The administration rejected the plan out of hand as being "inflammatory."[8] The NFD response to fire emergencies during a civil disturbance would differ little from any other day. Fire Chief Joseph Redden attempted to secure police protection for fire department responses in the event some disturbance occurred. He was informed that, "providing they could, they would provide us with Police protection."[9] This protection would be important because most of the apparatus used by the department had open cabs and no crew cab. A captain and a driver sat with the windshield in front of them and the sky above. Other members of the crew either stood on the back step of the engine companies or clung to the sides of the truck companies.

---

[6] Fire Chief Joe Redden, interview by Neal Stoffers, 16 September 2002, transcript. (Hereafter Redden). New Jersey State Archives Transcript of the Governor's Commission, booklet 14, 55, 24 October 1967 testimony of Fire Director Caufield (Hereafter Caufield).
[7] Newark Fire Department Annual Report 1967, p. 14.
[8] Deputy Chief Ed Wall, interview by author, 13 September 2000, transcript. (Hereafter Wall)
[9] Redden.

In the weeks preceding the meltdown, people began to approach firefighters with warnings about an impending riot.[10] The firefighters also began to notice people who didn't belong in the area.[11] The spark that set this kindling of resentment off was struck on July 12 when an African-American cab driver named John Smith was arrested and brought to the Fourth Precinct on Seventeenth and Belmont avenues.[12]

The Reverend William P. Hayes Homes housing project that loomed over this precinct was situated between Six Engine on Springfield Avenue and Twelve Engine on Belmont Avenue. Smith had to be carried from the patrol car into the precinct. This was witnessed by many residents of the projects. Rumors began to spread that the Police had beaten him to death. A crowd started to gather outside the precinct. Smith was taken out a back door and transported to Beth Israel Hospital where injuries to his head and ribs were treated. Police then attempted to disperse the crowd with only limited success. Molotov cocktails were hurled at the precinct when community activists encouraged the crowd to go home. Police officers were then sent out of the precinct with helmets and nightsticks. They encircled the building and faced the angry crowd. Racial epithets were exchanged between the groups and an abandoned car was set on fire.[13]

---

[10] Dunn. Wall. Freda.
[11] Dunn. F/F James Smith, interview by author, 30 June 1995, transcript. (Hereafter Smith)
[12] Belmont Ave has since been renamed Irvine Turner Blvd.
[13] Governor's Select Commission on Civil Disorder. *Report for Action.* (Trenton: 1968), p. 106-109. (Hereafter Governor's Commission)

Thursday July 13

At 12:10 A.M. Twelve Engine, Five Truck, and Salvage Two responded from their firehouse on Belmont and Waverly Avenues to the corner of Belmont and Seventeenth Avenues.[14] They turned west on to Seventeenth Avenue. The second tour was working the first of two consecutive nights.[15] When they left quarters they were told, "'Be prepared. There's a problem.' But nobody knew exactly what that problem was until we got there."[16] As Twelve Engine rolled in to the fire, the crowd parted to let them reach the burning car. The firefighters stretched a booster hose off the rig. Then there was a shout of "Get them!"[17]

When that happened then bricks and everything started raining from the project which loomed . . . right over the precinct. When this started occurring the Police ran inside the precinct, shut the door, and left the firemen out there by themselves. So, naturally there was a strategic withdrawal . ... The firemen jumped on the rig; the Captain jumped in; and they took off trailing the booster behind them . ...[18]

Six Engine was dispatched to assist Twelve Engine at 12:28 A.M. Before they rolled out of quarters, their Battalion Chief warned them "We might have a riot on our hands, so you better be a little careful."[19] Six Engine responded from their quarters on Springfield Avenue and Hunterdon Street and turned east onto Seventeenth Avenue. By the

---

[14] Waverly Avenue has since been renamed Muhammad Ali Avenue.

[15] At the time, the NFD had four tours or shifts that worked a forty-two hour week on an eight day rotation. Each tour worked two ten hour days, followed by forty-eight hours off and then two fourteen hour nights followed by seventy-two hours off. Approximately two hundred ten men were assigned to each tour.

[16] Captain William Harris, interview by author, 13 December 1999, transcript. (Hereafter Harris)

[17] Freda.

[18] Freda.

[19] Deputy Chief William Carragher, interview by author, November 1994, transcript. (Hereafter Carragher)

time the company arrived, Twelve Engine had fled. The police had come out of the precinct in helmets and were again surrounding the building. A large number of people were on the project roof and lawn. Before the Captain could get off the rig and ask the police what they needed, the company was bombarded with bricks and bottles. Fortunately, Six Engine's rig was one of the few in the city with a roof. When a rock the size of a basketball was thrown from the project roof, it hit the roof of the cab leaving a large indentation above the driver's head. Six Engine continued up Seventeenth Avenue and returned to quarters.[20] At 12:40 A.M, the first Deputy Chief had a special message broadcast over the fire department radio warning all members who responded to the first deputy division to wear their helmets.[21] Agitated crowds flowed down Springfield Avenue and Williams Street to Broad Street. When the crowd passed a firefighter in his private car, they shook it violently before moving on.[22] Companies were stoned on runs along Springfield Avenue for the rest of the night.[23]

The fourth tour relieved the second tour at 8:00 A.M. There was no unusual fire activity during the following day. The chiefs coming on duty were given no special instructions. The city was quiet when the second tour came in at 6 P.M. for their second night, but members

[20] Carragher. Firefighter Fred Charpentier, interview by author, 22 August 1993, transcript, (Hereafter Charpentier).

[21]Company Journals, Engine Companies 6, 10, 14, 19, 27, Truck Companies 1, 3, 4, 6, 10, Salvage Company 1, Fireboat 1, July 1967 (hereafter cited as Company Journals).

[22] Battalion Chief Al Payne, interview by author, 18 August 2004. As a firefighter, Chief Payne was on light duty watching a gas station with a leaking tank at the end of Springfield Avenue on the night of July 12-13.

[23] Freda.

reporting for duty were told to expect a riot. The word around the firehouse was it would begin at 8:00.[24]

In preparation truck companies were ordered to remove any tools from the rig that were not in compartments. Battalion Chiefs went to the firehouses and told their men how they were to operate in a civil disturbance. These instructions consisted of orders that fires were to be fought with 2½" lines in an attempt for a "quick knock-down and containment . . . and a minimum of overhauling . . . ."[25] Apparatus were to set up for a rapid exit from the scene if the situation outside a fire building became untenable. While firehouse doors were to be closed with personnel staying inside and out of view. When out of quarters, they were to avoid contact with rioters and were not to react to any taunts. A reduced assignment or "task force" would be dispatched to any alarms received after 6:00 P.M.[26]

At 6:45 P.M. there was a small picket line in front of the Fourth Precinct that gradually grew in length and attracted attention. By 7:30 approximately three hundred spectators were watching the picketers, but the police went about their business unmolested.[27] At about 8:00, "a heavy barrage of rocks, stones, bottles, and pieces of wood and metal hit the front of the precinct."[28] These objects were thrown over

---

[24] Carragher.

[25] Governor's Commission, Exhibit C-24, p. 1. "Overhauling" or de-construction as some texts call it, is a process of looking for hidden fire by pulling off the wall and ceiling lathe and plaster or wall board to expose the joists and studs of the fire building.

[26] A normal assignment was four engines companies, two trucks companies, a salvage company, a battalion chief, and a deputy chief. If there were a confirmed fire, then a rescue squad would be dispatched. The reduced assignment was patterned after the response of the Los Angles Fire Department task force responses during the Watts riots of 1965 and consisted of two engines, one truck, and one Battalion Chief. This assignment had the alarm designation of a Signal Nine and was rarely used before this with only 103 being transmitted in 1966.

[27]Governor's Commission, p. 112.

[28] *Ibid*, p. 113.

the picketers by the crowd behind them and caused the former to flee. Police going out to deal with the situation, broke up the crowd.

As the area around the precinct settled down, Springfield Avenue was heating up. At about the same time the first barrage of rocks and bottles rained down on the Fourth Precinct, the men of Six Engine watched a car stop in front of a jewelry store across from their quarters. Two men jumped out of the car and broke the jewelry store window. Before they could go into the store, three men with helmets and clubs came out after them. The would-be thieves fled, but looting began to spread up and down the avenue.[29] Fire Chief Redden was driving to a promotion dinner at one the firehouses in the Ironbound section of the city when he heard reports of looting on Springfield Avenue. He turned around and responded to Six Engine's quarters. Redden notified Fire Director John Caufield, who also responded to Six Engine. The men were speaking with members of the company next to a window on the apparatus floor that overlooked Springfield Avenue. They watched as a window was broken in Flax's Baby Furniture store a block east of the firehouse and a Molotov cocktail was thrown in. Six quickly rolled out of quarters. The first fire of the Newark riots had been set.

Although it required three task forces, the men were able to get a quick knock down of the fire with out any harassment. Alarms began flooding into fire dispatch. There were major fires on Hunterdon Street, Prince Street, Bergen Street, and Broad Street. Companies were calling in available from one fire only to be immediately assigned to another. Most of the fires were in the riot area. The only

---

[29] Carragher.

9

major fire that was an exception occurred at 805 Broad Street where a backdraft nearly killed several firefighters.[30]

Adding to the inherent danger of fighting fires, the rioters had begun throwing things. Rocks and bottles shattered the windshield of Truck Ten as they responded across Bergen Street, showering glass onto the Captain and driver.[31] Responding on Springfield Avenue, Salvage One's rig was also damaged.[32] When Twelve Engine, Five Truck, and Salvage Two responded to a fire on Prince Street, they were bombarded with rocks and bottles. Rioters surrounded the three pieces of apparatus before some of the neighborhood people stepped in. If the fire department was not allowed do its job, their homes were threatened.[33]

---

[30] Carragher. Charpentier. Deputy Chief Al McGrory, interview by author, 31 August 1991, transcript. (Hereafter McGrory) A backdraft or smoke explosion occurs when oxygen is suddenly introduced into an environment that has heat and fuel but cannot burn freely because it lacks oxygen.
[30] Newark Fire Department, Company Journal Truck 10, July 1967. (Hereafter Truck 10)
[31] Newark Fire Department, Company Journal Salvage 1 July 1967. (Hereafter Salvage 1)
[33] Harris.

Friday July 14

The situation continued to deteriorate. By 1:30 A.M., Fire Chief Redden ordered a recall of off duty personnel and emergency procedures were put in place. All two-piece engine companies were to divide themselves between the two apparatus and respond separately.[34] Members reporting on the recall filled in with the two-piece companies or manned spare apparatus and responded where needed. This increased the number of engine companies available for fire duty from twenty-five to forty. [35] The number was decreased by one at 12:36 when one of Engine Nineteen's apparatus was damaged in a collision with a car on High and Spruce streets while responding to an alarm. Tragically, a woman lost her life in this accident.[36] Even with the recall, the city had to request mutual aid from Elizabeth, Irvington, Belleville, and East Orange.[37] The out of town companies were quickly put to work.

After the rioting spread to Springfield Avenue, Fire Chief Redden responded to Police Headquarters to request protection. When Redden arrived at City Hall, he walked into an office busy ordering equipment needed to handle a riot. The Newark Police could not provide the protection he sought. Firefighters would not see consistent protection until the National Guard was assigned that duty early on July 16. [38] Mayor Addonizio called Governor Richard Hughes at 2:20 A.M. to

---

[34] At the time the Newark Fire Department had ten companies that rode with two apparatus. The primary rig was a thousand gallon pumper. The second truck did not have as high a pumping capacity and was referred to as the "hose wagon." This terminology was a throw back to the horse drawn days when the steamers did not carry hose. All engine companies had two pieces, the steamer for moving water and the hose wagon for carrying and stretching the hose.
[35] Governor's Commission, Caufield testimony, booklet 14, p. 60.
[36] Governor's Commission, p. 138-139.
[37] Newark Fire Department Annual Report, 1967, p. 24.
[38] Redden. Company Journals.

request state police and National Guard assistance.[39] Elements of the state police arrived in Newark about 5:30 A.M.,[40] and as its forces grew they gradually took over the patrol duties in the riot area.

The National Guard began reporting from various parts of the state later in the day; 3,464 guardsmen were assigned to Newark at the end of the day. Of these, 1,749 were from suburban and rural areas of the state.[41] The guard unit assigned to the Roseville armory in North Newark was at Fort Drum.[42] They would not be assigned to duty in Newark until July 17. Units from the Newark vicinity would return to their armories for meals and rest after a three-to-four hour tour. Other units set up a base in City Stadium. Troops were issued a small number of metal jacketed bullets before being deployed. They would receive more rounds in the field.[43]

Noticeably absent that first night was gunfire; only one instance of sniping was reported. At 8:00 A.M. the fourth tour officially reported for duty. Many of the men were already working, having been called in during the night. A number of those stationed in the Central Ward firehouses did not return home for days because they did not want to risk the ride from firehouse to home and back. Command responsibility shifted to the officers of the on-coming tour. All the chief officers were summoned to a meeting in fire headquarters at 8:02 and were told to take all necessary precautions.

---

[39] Governor's Commission, p. 115.
[40] Governor's Commission, p. 116.
[41] Governor's Commission, exhibit C-20: Operational Report of the New Jersey National Guard, Newark, N.J., Period 14 thru 17 July 1967.
[42] Wall.
[43] Captain John Rosamilia, interview by author, 19 August 2004.

It was after 10:00 A.M. when Six Engine returned to their quarters from the Broad Street fire. The state police were on Springfield Avenue.[44] Even with the state police presence, looting continued along the avenue. Governor Hughes toured the area and was appalled by the lawlessness that was taking place in a "holiday atmosphere."[45] He signed an emergency proclamation shortly after 9:30 Friday morning. Along with the proclamation were regulations prohibiting vehicular traffic between 10 P.M. and 6 A.M., the sale or possession of alcoholic beverages, and the possession of firearms or explosives. An 11 P.M. to 6 A.M. curfew was also imposed.[46] The police decided to cordon off the riot area. By Friday evening the center of the city was isolated.

Unusually heavy fire activity continued throughout the day. Firefighters responded to their old neighborhoods to fight fires.[47] Responses entailed anything from burning trash to working fires in commercial occupancies. On West Runyon Street, a block of businesses was burnt out. There were major fires on Hawthorne Avenue and Bergen Street, on Springfield and Morris Avenues, and on Clinton Avenue.[48]

Chiefs instructed their men to avoid confrontations. Companies were told not to respond through the areas around the Newark Housing Authority projects scattered throughout the Central Ward. These were seen as hotbeds of discontent. During the day, there were

---

[44] Carpentier. Carragher.
[45] US News and World Report, July 24, 1967, p.6.
[46] Governor's Commission, p. 117.
[47] Firefighter Gerald Highsmith, interview by author, 2 June 1994, transcript. (Hereafter Highsmith)
[48] Company Journals.

few problems with the citizens. Although fires were set, neighborhood people would "help you do everything you could possibly want them to do with no problem."[49] The vast majority of the people continued to respect the firefighters. "If you got the cops there, that's when they started acting up, testing them. Of course, you're in the middle, but that happened all the time, it just carried through during the riots."[50] The looting continued even while firefighters were stretching hoses and pouring water into buildings. Because the fire department has no arresting authority, all the firefighters could do was warn the looters of possible injury if they went into a fire building.[51]

Acting Deputy Chief Fred Grehl was asked by fire headquarters to go into the field and get a feel for the situation.

> They said, "You have a good rapport with these people in this neighborhood." I had been in this area my whole life. "Go out and see what the feelings are out there." I'm talking to this one guy, he says, "See that watermelon wagon over there. When he leaves that means all hell's gonna break loose." So, I says, "What time do you expect him to leave?" He says, "About five o'clock." "Oh." So, I report that downtown. They don't believe me.[52]

By 4:00 Friday afternoon, it was obvious that the fire situation was not going to improve. At 4:40 companies were informed that effective the six o'clock roll call manpower would be:

---

[49] Highsmith.
[50] Deputy Chief Fred Grehl, interview by Neal Stoffers, 7 August 1993, transcript. (Hereafter Grehl)
[51] Grehl.
[52] Grehl.

- Two piece companies – two Captains and two tours, each piece to ride as a single company

- Single piece companies – one Captain and six men, no acting officers

The extra personnel needed to fill out this roll call would come from tour four, who would work with tour three for the night. Additionally, members of tour four would man four spare apparatus. These would ride from firehouses outside the riot area.[53]

The assignment of six firefighters to single piece companies led to some very crowded apparatus. Since firefighters normally clung to the sides or aerial ladders of the truck companies, these were not really affected. Ordinarily, the back steps of the engine companies were crowded with four firefighters on them. With the increased roll calls, one or two men had to ride on top of the hose beds in the single-piece companies when the engine rolled out of quarters.[54]

Men coming to work at the firehouses in the Central Ward were told to report to specified locations where they would pickup a police escort. Anyone coming into the Central Ward from the north was to stop at the Roseville Avenue Armory. Men coming in from Vailsburg were to stop at the Vailsburg firehouse first. Unfortunately, any men living in the area of unrest had to fend for themselves unescorted.[55]

---

[53] Company journals. This schedule effectively put the department on an 84 hour work week. Two tours would be working at any given time. The spare apparatus were sent to a firehouse in the Vailsburg section of the city, a firehouse in the Ironbound, and the Special Service house (2 engines) also Downneck.

[54] Charpentier.

[55] Charpentier. Freda. Harris. Deputy Chief Jim McCormack, interview by author, 14 June 1991, transcript. (Hereafter McCormick)

15

On Friday evening the tone of the riots began to change. Where the night before there was no gunfire to speak of, at 5:00 shots began to ring out around Six Engine on Springfield Avenue. Battalion Chief Ed Wall was leaving the quarters Battalion Four shared with that company.

At that time the street was Belgian blocks. I saw sparks coming off the blocks. We took off. (My driver) said, "What?" I said, "There's somebody shooting at us." We come back. The state police sergeant says, to me, "Do you know where they were shooting at you from?" I said, "I have no idea." He took me in the alley. He showed me the window. The window is right across from the chief's room. You can still see the bullet holes there.[56]

After a sniper began firing from an eighth-floor window of the projects across from the firehouse, Six Engine and Battalion Four went out of service. The watermelon truck had left the area and all hell was about to break loose.

Deputy Chief Al Freda, a captain at Twelve Engine at the time, knew what was happening in the Central Ward. He decided to car pool with two other men from North Newark. Chief Ryan and Lenny Mendola, who both worked in Six Engine, met me at my house because we had heard the radio reports that there was a riot taking place. So we went to the Armory on Roseville Avenue. Chief Ryan went inside and asked for an escort to our firehouses. I waited in my Volkswagen mini bus. Chief Ryan came out with four or five state policemen. Two of them got right in the mini bus with shotguns. They put a state police car in front of us, one behind us, and off we

---

[56] Wall.

16

went. Our plan was to drop Lenny and the Chief at Six Engine. Then I would continue on to Twelve Engine, which was not a far distance away. I felt as safe as I ever felt in my life. We stopped at Six Engine. We were there no more than a minute. We really didn't have a handle on how bad things were. The policemen on the apron were waving at us. I didn't know why they were waving. We were looking at them. They're making all kinds of hand gestures and waving. Just then two bullets ricocheted off the apron at Six Engine. They apparently came from the projects. When this happened, naturally panic ensued inside the van. The state troopers jumped out. The cops took off for the firehouse because they're out in the open. I was trying to coax Ryan and Mendola urgently to get the hell out of my van so I can get out of there. I'll never forget it because Ryan got out and Mendola was stumbling to get his lunch. He was bent down. I pushed him out of the mini bus with my foot and took off with his lunch, which was good, because I had lunch that night. I ate his lunch. I took off for the firehouse. I mean as fast as the bus could go. When I got to Twelve Engine, that particular area at that time was very quiet.[57]

The quiet on Belmont Avenue did not last long. More people would be killed by gunfire in the next fourteen hours than in any other period in the disturbances. The holiday atmosphere the Governor described would die with them. For Newark firefighters, worries of snipers and stray bullets supplanted the concerns of fighting fires. Detective Fred Toto of the Newark Police was shot late in the

---

[57] Freda.

afternoon. Blood donations for him were requested over the fire department radio. Firefighters stopped at Saint Michael's Hospital to give before reporting for duty.[58]

The men coming on duty came into a city in crisis. By now the state police had assumed the patrol duties in the riot area. The National Guard had barbed wire fences across Springfield Avenue and Twentieth Street and had sealed off 136 other intersections.[59] Some of the personnel coming on duty immediately went to fire scenes to relieve working crews. A small but significant indication that chaos reigned in the city was the absence of a time blow[60] at the 6:00 P.M. change of tours. Alarms and fires continued to flow into fire dispatch. Now reports of gunfire accompanied the reports of fires.

Twelve Engine rolled up to a heavy fire condition at 95 Prince Street shortly after 6:30. The Scudder Homes housing project towered over the area. While the company was deciding how best to attack the fire, shots rang out from the projects. "I remember the windows start breaking in the fire building and I thought for a second, 'Gee, I didn't think anybody went in there yet and here they're ventilating.' For that second, but in the next second I figured out it was bullets hitting the windows and breaking the windows."[61] The firefighters quickly stretched 2½ inch hose into the building, did a

---

[58] Battalion Chief John Ryan, in discussion with author, 18 August 2004.
Detective Toto died later that evening.
[59] Governor's Commission, p. 118.
[60]At 8 A.M. and again at 6 P.M. a single bell was sent over the telegraph
system to all the firehouses in the city. This "blow" on the bell
announced the time and signified the change of tour. The time blow was
accompanied by a radio announcement which included the list of chief officers on duty and
any special announcements ordered by the Fire Chief or Director.
[61] Freda.

minimal amount of overhauling, and left. While there, they saw another fire around the corner and called it in. For the next two nights, many companies used 2½ inch hose lines that were laid on top of the apparatus and pre-connected to the pump panel. They "would go in very quickly and knock these fires down and drown the building."[62]

Fire companies attempted to insulate themselves from the rioters. The black firefighters noticed that, "white guys wanted to be close to you then."[63] Firefighters heard stories of black police officers being harassed by other cops, but on "the fire department, we didn't have any problems between firemen. In fact what was being said was, 'Hey, we got any black guys riding on the rig tonight?' or 'We got any guys over here?'"[64] The Captain at Twelve Engine thought it would be best if he sat between two black firefighters in the cab of the rig. On the first run of the night, the company was greeted with shouts of "Get those Uncle Toms." Rocks and bottles accompanied the verbal abuse, so the company went back to their usual response routine.[65]

Amid the chaos that enveloped the center of the city, a thread of normalcy was woven. Firehouses continued to be aid stations. Women in labor came to them for assistance. Injured citizens did likewise. If the injured were not in the vicinity of a firehouse, they pulled fire boxes on the street. Responses to accidental car fires and unattended cooking also continued. The only difference was the sound of gunfire in the background.[66]

---

[62]Freda.

[63] Firefighter Boisey Cosby, interview by author, 17 June 2003, tape recording.

[64] Harris.

[65] Freda.

19

Not surprisingly given the atmosphere they were working in, firefighters began to carry weapons. Not all of them had training in their use. This led to some close calls in firehouses around the city, but there were no injuries from misfired weapons. One of the more surreal incidents involving gunfire occurred in Seventeen Engine on Clinton Place. Firefighters were in the basement testing their guns. They were using tracer bullets, firing at targets against a wall. Below the targets was a table with old turnout gear piled on it. In the middle of their practice the company responded to a fire. When they returned, a fire was burning freely in the basement. The tracer rounds had ignited the old turnout gear. Company members quickly extinguished the fire.[67]

The firefighters carried guns exclusively for self-defense, and they never felt more vulnerable than when they responded to the projects. By the time an alarm came in for the Scudder Homes housing project, Twelve Engine and Five Truck had already devised a plan for protection. They decided that two men would stay at either end of the corridor with revolvers drawn while the companies worked on the fire. If anyone opened an apartment door, an order would be barked out to close the door. "The odd thing about it, we never encountered any bad feelings in the projects." Deputy Chief Freda stated. "Nobody bothered us or anything. There was sniper fire and I always felt it was a plan to cause this type of atmosphere."[68]

---

[66] Company Journals of Engine 6 and Engine 10, July, 1967.
[67] Captain William Brownlee, interview by author, 30 August 2004, recounting the story told him when he was assigned to Seventeen Engine. The fire in Seventeen's basement was well known around the NFD, but the story had been embellished. Instead of old turnout coats burning, it was said that the furnace was pierced by a bullet causing the fire. A table is still in the basement complete with burn marks and a blackened ceiling.

The atmosphere brought back memories of combat to some of the World War II and Korean War veterans. Since neither the police nor the National Guard were providing protection to the fire department, the firefighters felt justified in arming themselves. The weapons they carried were not limited to side-arms. When a group of men armed with knives and axes approached Ten Engine at a fire and told the pump operator to stop flowing water, one firefighter produced a carbine to prevent any interference. Fortunately, there were no incidents of firefighters shooting anyone. Fire Headquarters heard of the situation and quickly issued orders forbidding the carrying of arms by firefighters.[69]

Throughout the night, companies continued to respond to alarms for large and small fires, but the fire situation did not reach the levels of the previous night. The twenty-four hour period from 6:00 Friday evening to 6:00 Saturday evening saw seventy-one fires, down from the 122 fires of the previous night.[70] There were major fires on Prince Street, Scott Street, and Bergen Street.[71] The Scott Street fire was the only major fire outside the primary riot zone. A food market on Orchard Street was hit with two Molotov cocktails, but only a minor fire ensued that was quickly extinguished. As the night progressed, the weapons fire grew worse.

---

[68] Freda.
[69] Smith. Freda. Deputy Chief Richard Bitter, interview by author, 27 December 2002, tape recording.
[70] Governor's Commission, p. 125
[71] Company journals.

Saturday July 15

Five Truck responded to a false alarm at Avon Avenue and Bergen Street shortly after midnight. While returning to quarters a bullet went through both of the twin tires on the tractor of the truck. The tires could not be repaired in their firehouse or the area surrounding it, so the truck was driven to Broad Street. Mechanics met the truck there and changed the tires under a streetlight. The company responded back into the riot zone. By the end of the night they had responded to twenty-six alarms and the firefighters felt they had been shot at on each response.[72]

When roll call was conducted at 8:00 Saturday morning, nerves were frayed, but no fires were burning. Fire department roll calls during the day dropped down to a more normal compliment of one officer and four men. The number of alarms continued to decline, but the city remained an armed camp. Fewer than twenty alarms were transmitted over the fire department circuits throughout the day.[73] Sporadic looting continued, with at least one instance of the activity moving away from the riot area.[74] As the 6:00 P.M. time blow approached, an announcement was transmitted over the radio that roll calls would be beefed up again for the night. At a little after 5:00 a Molotov cocktail was thrown onto the roof of 117 Pennington Street, which caused a small fire that was quickly extinguished. Molotov cocktails continued to be thrown, but they were no longer the primary concern of the firefighters.

---

[72] Bitter.

[73] Company Journals.

[74] A citizen came into Six Truck in North Newark to request a police response to Broadway and Oriental Street for looting. Company Journal Truck 6, July 1967.

More than the previous night, gunfire became the paramount worry. Six Engine had become a state police command post early on. Even though the state police moved to the Pabst Brewing complex where the company was providing food to them,[75] Six Engine remained a target for snipers firing from the Hayes Homes across the street. At 6:30 the company went out of service again because of gunfire in the area. Battalion Four went out a minute later, Deputy Chief Jim McCormick recalled:

> There was so much shooting outside Six Engine. I mean guns going off; who was shooting at whom I had no way of knowing because we were in the firehouse, but it sounded like we were in a war zone. There were guns going off constantly, automatic weapon fire and single shots, shooting going constantly. I remember we were under the impression the shots were coming from the projects across the street. Because they're very high and they look down on the firehouse. At one point the shooting got so bad that I wouldn't let Six Engine respond. I kept them in the firehouse until the police moved in and more or less stabilized the area.[76]

Two hours passed before the chief felt the area was stable enough for Six Engine to roll out of their quarters. Six was not the only company in the Fourth Battalion to receive gunfire, nor was the Fourth Battalion's area the only one in the city under fire.

Central Avenue had been relatively calm, with only three alarms transmitted for fireboxes along it. It was the northern most border of the area (twenty-four by thirty-six blocks) the National Guard considered the trouble zone.[77] Some time before 10:00 on Friday

[75] Deputy Chief Grehl in discussion with author July 21 2004.
[76] McCormack.
[77] Governor's Commission, exhibit C-20: Operational Report of the New Jersey National Guard, Newark, N.J., Period 14 thru 17 July 1967.

evening a car sped up the avenue. Firefighters in the firehouse on Central Avenue and Ninth Street heard a large volume of gunfire and dove to the floor.[78] The weapons fire set off a sequence of events that would take the life of one of Newark's bravest.

At 10:14 an alarm was received for Station 6155 indicating water was flowing from a sprinkler system at 500 Central Avenue between South Seventh Street and South Eighth Street. Engine Eleven, Engine Seven, and Battalion One responded. Director Caufield also rode in because of the reports of gunfire in the area. National Guardsmen and police officers were lined up along the avenue from Tenth Street to Seventh Street.

There was no sign of a fire when the companies pulled up. No water was flowing from the building. Engine Eleven investigated the front of the building while Engine Seven and Battalion One went around to the back. A National Guardsman challenged the chief when he reached the back, but after flashing his light to show his helmet, the chief lent the guardsman the light so he could look through a playground behind the building.

While the chief was in the rear of the building, Captain Michael Moran from Eleven Engine decided not to force entry through the front door because this would leave the building open to looters. Instead a ladder would be thrown up to a second-floor window and entry made through it. The ladder would be used to break the window,

---

[78]Deputy Chief David Kinnear, interview by author, 28 September 1992, transcript. (Hereafter Kinnear) The origin of the gunfire is still in question. The men in the firehouse thought it sounded like automatic weapons fire, but when the car crashed there was no weapon recovered. One of the two occupants was arrested and held as a material witness to murder. He was subsequently released after paying a fine for violating curfew.

minimizing the exposure of fire personnel. Captain Moran stood on one side of the ladder. Director Caufield stood opposite him. Firefighters raised the ladder and dropped it into the window. "As soon as the ladder hit that window and made a noise," Ray McGee, a firefighter at the time at Seven Engine stated, "all hell started, all shooting started and continued for maybe fifteen or twenty seconds."[79] Everyone dove to the ground and tried to find cover until an order was shouted to cease firing.

Captain Moran and a National Guardsman had been hit. A metallic 30-06 bullet had entered Moran through the abdomen and had lodged in his pelvis.[80] There were no ambulances available, so the Captain was quickly carried to the Battalion Chief's car and the guardsman to the director's car. Two firefighters jumped in the Chief's gig and raced to Presbyterian Hospital. The Battalion Chief remained on the scene to organize the men and get them out of the area.[81] Captain Moran died of his wounds on the way to the hospital.[82] Controversy still surrounds the source of the bullet. Whatever its source, Michael Moran gave his life performing his sworn duty, protecting the lives and property of the citizens of Newark. The guardsman survived the ordeal.

---

[79] Captain Ray McGee, interview by author, 26 October 2000, transcript. (Hereafter McGee)
[80] Caufield, p. 139.
[81] Kinnear. Firefighters William Knispel and James Kavanaugh drove Captain Moran to the hospital.
[82] Caufield, p. 72.

Sunday July 16

The fire department reacted quickly to the shooting. A radio message was broadcast instructing units not to enter areas where gunfire was reported. Companies were told not to respond with lights and sirens. By 1:30 A.M. Salvage One was transporting National Guardsmen to firehouses throughout the city. They would not return to quarters until after 7:00 A.M.[83]

In other parts of the city shooting incidents affecting the fire department had increased dramatically. At 12:14 A.M. Twelve Engine came under fire while backing into their quarters after returning from an alarm. When a bullet hit the rig, the crew had to abandon it in the middle of the street and seek cover in the firehouse. What happened next only increased the anxiety of the firefighters.

> When we first abandoned the rig the National Guard, the state police, and the Newark Police showed up and were lined up across three aprons, two deep with every conceivable weapon you could think of. They had gotten the message because the communication was bad that the firehouse was under siege when all we did was get shot at. "Under siege" meant, we were captured by the enemy. The Polish woman who lived (across the street) on the third floor looked out the window and they opened up on her apartment. The roar was so deafening that you couldn't hear the individual shots. It sounded like one continuous roar. You couldn't distinguish between individual weapons. I ran out and tried to tell them that an old woman was living there. But they couldn't even hear me. One guy pushed me and didn't want to listen. I thought the woman was dead. I would say without exaggeration there were a thousand rounds shot into her apartment. Now we weren't going in there by ourselves. They all left. They didn't even check. The next day this woman's son came down (to Newark). The son came down

---

(from the apartment) and he came toward the firehouse. My heart was in my throat because I thought he was going to tell me this woman was dead. He says, "What happened last night?" I started to tell him, but he interrupted me. He says, "My mother said." Then I knew she was alive and I calmed down. He said, "I found my mother under the bed in the back room and she won't come out. Everything in the apartment is broken. All the tile on the kitchen wall is off the wall, broken, every light bulb, every glass, every lamp, everything that's breakable is broken. There's nothing standing that could break. It's broken and she won't come out." So, I told him what happened, but I was relieved that woman wasn't dead.[84]

Warnings against responding to areas of heavy gunfire were recorded in company journals at 12:35 and again at 1:55. All Battalion Chiefs were ordered to the Roseville Armory at 2:30. By 3:35, only Battalion Chiefs were responding to alarms. They would investigate and call for additional companies if needed. As the sun rose over the city, word was going around to the men in her firehouses that one of their own had died.[85]

The first tour relieved the third tour. Announcements ordering companies to leave any scene if fired upon were again broadcast over the fire department frequency. By 10:30, Battalion Chiefs were ordering flags to be flown at half-mast. It was not until just before the 6:00 time blow that the four fours[86] where transmitted over the bell system announcing the passing of Captain Michael Moran. The fourth tour relieved the first tour.

---

[84] Freda. The sidewalk and driveway in front of a firehouse are referred to as the "apron."
[85] Company Journals.
[86] The signal over the alarm system that a firefighter has been killed in the line of duty is four groups of four bells.

National Guardsmen were now in all the firehouses. At times this in itself presented problems.[87] The troops now responding with fire companies were for the most part young and inexperienced.[88] This was the first time New Jersey National Guard troops had been deployed to quell a civil disturbance.[89] They had received riot training that was appropriate to situations involving large crowds. They had received no training on dealing with sniper situations.

Many of these men were from suburban and rural New Jersey; they had little exposure to an urban setting, as Captain William Harris stated:

> Ninety percent of them I would say never lived or experienced being around blacks. They would come into the firehouse and say little things. In Twelve Engine, we had one black police officer, Charlie. He was there. He was a motorcycle cop. He was stationed with us that night with this other police officer. They got into a big row with the National Guard people because they were saying things. "We need to go out and blow those people up. And we need to do this and we need to do that."

> They said, "Ho, I'm one of those people you're talking about, but I'm wearing this badge and I'm going to do this job. But I don't have to sit here and let you say these things." We had National Guard after them, but I didn't see those guys anymore and we didn't hear these comments anymore.[90]

---

[87]Company Journals.

[88] In his testimony before the Governor's Commission, General James F. Cantwell of the Guard (Hereafter Cantwell) stated that the "average" age of National Guardsmen assigned to Newark was 24. He does not state whether this "average" is a mean, median, or mode. He also does not state what the "average"age of the soldiers assigned to patrol duty was. All firefighters I have nterviewed are in agreement on the youth of these men.

[89]Cantwell, October 20, 1967, p. 6.

[90]Harris.

The National Guard Troops were "young and very scared."[91] To Newark firefighters, most of whom were veterans,[92] they presented yet another danger to be dealt with. One Captain found it necessary to disarm a guardsman because whenever he heard a shot, the young man would charge into the firehouse with rifle bayonet fixed, unsheathed, and at his waist in a horizontal position. After being warned to stop or he would injure or kill one of the firefighters he was supposed to be protecting, the Captain felt obliged to relieve the Guardsman of his weapon. The Guard sergeant did not find the confiscation of government property by a Newark fire captain amusing.[93]

Companies were now responding with state police and National Guard escorts. Convoys were formed when the Battalion Chief called for additional help. These could include National Guard armor vehicles and state police cruisers.[94]

Crews had again reverted to their normal compliment during the day. Even though with "the coming of daybreak on Sunday, tensions seemed to ease," companies were still beefed up in anticipation of more troubles that night.[95] The number of fires had continued to decrease from the peak levels of the first night, dropping to 34 the third night of rioting.[96]

---

[91] National Commission, p. 67.
[92] New Jersey Civil Service laws allowed any veteran who passed a civil service test to be placed at the top of a civil service list. Only after the veterans were hired would other non-veterans be considered.
[93] Freda.
[94] Bitter.
[95] Commission, p. 123. Company Journals.
[96] Caufield, C-24.

Fires and fire department responses decreased further. No fires developed beyond one task force, with only twenty-three fires reported the entire night. The disturbance appeared to be calming. The riot area remained sealed off. Battalion Chiefs continued to respond to alarms to investigate; other companies "responded" on stand by in their quarters.

Monday July 17

On Monday morning the tours changed at 8:00 and manpower reverted back to normal. At 8:55, units were told that responses on alarms would be answered by task forces until 6:00.

Starting at 1:30, firefighters were detailed to the Burns Funeral Home on Sanford Avenue to stand honor guard for Captain Moran. Department Notice 77 announcing his death was delivered to the firehouses that afternoon. By 3:30 National Guard trucks were picking guardsmen up from firehouses. The state police and National Guard were pulling out of Newark.[97]

After the evening time blow, the announcement about leaving any location where there was gunfire was repeated.[98] This was followed by an invitation to all off-duty personnel who would like to say the Rosary for the repose of the soul of Captain Michael Moran to report to the Burns Funeral Home at 8:00 P.M. Fire companies only responded to fifteen alarms citywide that night.[99]

Newark began its excruciating recovery from the riots that Monday. For the fire department, it started with small gestures.

We came back in our first day on Monday and the riots had settled down a little bit. I remember going up to a box. We were about one and six then and went out with the state police, the National Guard, and the Chief. There was something small. We came back and then they said, "Well, it looks like everything is over. It's quieting down." So we decided right then and there, "Okay, let's open the door up. Open the firehouse," because everything was barricaded. "Let's open the firehouse up. Let's get the rig out." There was a staging area for the state police and the National Guard

---

[97] Company Journals. Commission, p. 124.
[98] Company Journals.
[99] *Ibid.*

in Six Engine. It was a mess. Everybody had ration cans laying all over the place and food wrapping. Garbage was piled all over. We cleaned the place up. We got the hose out, got all the garbage out, and hosed the place out. It was back to normal again that quick on a Monday.[100]

The Governor began to lift emergency restrictions at 3:00 P.M. on Monday. He lifted all restrictions on Wednesday, officially ending the Newark riots.[101] The fire department did not revert to normal running assignments until July 23 at the 8:00 A.M. time blow.[102]

Services for Captain Moran were held at Sacred Heart Church in Vailsburg on the evening of July 18, 1967. A plaque commemorating his sacrifice rides on Eleven Engine to this day. The investigation into his death proved inconclusive.

---

[100] Carragher.
[101] Commission, p. 124.
[102] Company Journals.

The Aftermath

The Newark Fire Department responded to 364 alarms in the ninety-six hour period between 6:00 in the evening of Thursday July 13 and 6:00 in the evening of Monday July 17. 250 of these alarms were responses to fires. Thirty-five firefighters were injured in the performance of their duty. Captain Michael Moran was killed; leaving behind a pregnant wife and six children. Snipers directed fire at fire department personnel, facilities, or apparatus thirty-three times during the last three nights of the disturbances.[103] According to historian Ron Porambo, "The gunfire directed at firehouses came from men who wanted a safe target, one that represented the power structure but was unarmed."[104] Property damage estimates approached 10.5 million dollars. Damaged or looted stock accounted for a little over 8 million dollars of these losses.[105]

The damage done by the July disturbances would prove cancerous for decades. Fires would rip through blocks, changing working class neighborhoods of three-story wooden tenements into vacant lots. In April 1968 on the day of Rev. Martin Luther King, Jr.'s funeral, fire consumed twenty-six buildings. Thirty-four buildings were vaporized in a firestorm on Avon Avenue and Bergen Street later that month.[106] The task forces of the riots were used to

---

[103]Notes of Chief Redden given to Battalion Chief Wall for his testimony before the National Advisory Commission on Civil Disorders.

[104] Ron Porambo, *No Cause for Indictment: An Autopsy of Newark*, New York, Holt, Rinefort and Winston, 1971, p. 132. (Hereafter Porambo.)

[105] New Jersey State Patrolmen's Benevolent Association , *The Road to Anarchy: Findings of the Riot Study Commission of the New Jersey PBA*, privately printed, p. 70.

[106] Stanley B. Winters, *From Riot to Recovery: Newark Ten Years After.*

deal with both of these events. The fire department adopted an emergency operating procedure for civil disturbances, considered too inflammatory before the riots, the following February and used it to coordinate the fire responses in April.

With the riots, the demographic and economic changes that had begun after World War II accelerated dramatically. Whole neighborhoods were transformed as the population of Newark became overwhelmingly African-American.

Central Avenue around the firehouse was a fairly stable, mostly Irish neighborhood before the riots. That changed after the riots. People were moving out prior to that, but they left in droves after the riots. This was done within two or three years, a major, major change.[107]

Businesses that were burnt out during the riots never returned, choosing to move to the suburbs. A rash of fires struck commercial properties whose owners claimed they had been firebombed. No one could prove otherwise. Relations with the citizens of the city also underwent a change.

The attitude of the firemen towards the people and the people towards the firemen changed. Before, we were very aggressive getting in there and after we were very cautious. Because a few incidents even after the riots where we were still being pelted by rocks and bricks. They were booby trapping buildings and sucking us in, cutting holes in the floor and putting linoleum or something over where you step. You'd go through the floor. Or they put nails through a piece

Washington,D.C.: University Press of America, 1979, p. 5. (Hereafter Winters)
The fire on Avon and Bergen occurred on April 20, 1968.
[107] McGee.

of wood that would come down when you opened a door. We had to be extra, extra careful for our own protection.[108]

Firefighters discussed whether the riots changed their attitudes toward the people they served. All agreed that as far as performing their job, there was no change. They would still do their utmost to save lives and protect property. Deputy Chief David Kinnear maintained that the riots caused changes "just in personal relationships, outside of firefighting, where you didn't feel they had the same respect for you that they had before."[109]

If the false alarm rate is used as a barometer of the respect people felt for firefighters, then a monumental shift came about after the riots. The number of malicious false alarms skyrocketed over the next fifteen years. In 1982 the Department responded to 10,640 "Signal 300's," up from 1,614 in 1966. A more telling statistic than the overall rate of false alarms is the rate from the Newark school system. In 1966 there were sixty-three false alarms transmitted to Newark schools. In 1967 there were one hundred twenty-three. Seventy-four of these were transmitted between September and December. The number of school false alarms shot up to 972 in 1975.[110] Even for school age children, there was a dramatic shift in attitudes towards summoning the fire department needlessly. Firefighter Fred Charpentier said:

For a long time after everything calmed down (the people) were very hostile to us. Before the riots, we were there to help. It seemed that during the riots and after the riots, people who were forty, fifty years old and up were still very good with us.

---

[108] Charpentier.
[109] Kinnear.
[110] Company Journals.

We had a good rapport with them, but the majority of those younger than forty were still hostile to us. We were their enemies.[111]

The fire rate continued to climb, ravishing the Central Ward. According to riot analyst Stanley Winters, during the next decade fires were "an enormous force in changing Newark."[112] Burnt-out buildings provided shelter for vagrants and drug addicts. Abandoned buildings became the playground of neighborhood children in the center of the city. These structures also had a high incidence of fire. The city began to systematically demolish unsafe structures in 1970. In the next seven years, over 7000 structures were torn down.[113] Demolition became "a necessary form of suicide"[114] and continued well into the next decade. The changing force that was fire reached its apex in 1980 when 725 major structural fires were reported. The following year, fire department responses reached their peak of 28,008.[115] The rate began a slow decent over the next two decades as Newark clawed its way back.[116] Political changes have addressed many of the complaints that precipitated the riots. Newark is now called the Renaissance City; no one now on her fire department experienced those four days in July.[117]

---

[111] Chapentier. This viewpoint varied depending on which firehouse a Firefighter was assigned. Men assigned to Central Ward firehouses were more likely to share this opinion.
[112] Winters, p. 5.
[113] *Ibid.*
[114] *Ibid.*
[115] Newark Fire Department Annual Reports 1958 –2002.
[116] Newark Fire Department Annual Reports 1958-2002.
[117] As of August 25, 2004 there was one firefighter still on the job who was appointed before July, 1967. He retired September 1, 2004.

"The fellows did a tremendous job," Deputy Chief Fred Grehl stated. "I couldn't believe the heroism because they said they weren't shooting at firemen, but . . . Captain (Moran) was killed."[118]

Porambo later declared, "During the course of the disorders members of the Newark Fire Department had been nothing short of heroic. It was they who took the brunt of the ghetto's anger."[119]

On July 24, 1967, Department Notice 81 was issued. Its subject was Executive Order 324. In it Fire Director Caufield wrote:

I witnessed so many courageous deeds that it would be impossible for me to single out the members to commend them individually; indeed, every member acted in the finest traditions of the Fire Department.[120]

[118] Grehl.
[119] Porambo, p. 121.
[120]Newark Fire Department Notice 81, July 24, 1967.

List of Interviewees:

Bitter, Deputy Chief Richard, 27 December 2002. Tape recording.

Brownlee, Captain William, in discussion with the author 30 August 2004.

Butler, Captain James, 3 September 1993, transcript.

Cahill, Firefighter Joseph, 25 June 1991, transcript.

Carragher, Deputy Chief William, November 1994, transcript.

Charpentier, Firefighter Frederick, 22 August 1993, transcript.

Cody, Battalion Chief James, 26 October 1999, transcript.

Cosby, Firefighter Boisey, 17 June 2003, transcript.

Denvir, Captain John, 13 September 1993, transcript.

Deutch, Firefighter Charles, 14 November 1993, transcript.

Dunn, Deputy Chief Edward, 14 August 1991, 29 August 1997, transcript.

Freda, Deputy Chief Alfred, 12, 25, 26 July 1991, transcript.

Freeman, Captain Richard, 20, 21 August 1991, transcript.

Garrity, Battalion Chief Joseph, May 1992, transcript.

Gaynor, Battalion Chief Robert, 22 October 1999, tape recording.

Grehl, Deputy Chief Frederick, 7 August 1993, transcript.

Haran, Captain Edward, 5 February 2001, transcript.

Harris, Captain William, 13 December 1999, transcript. .

Highsmith, Firefighter Gerald, 2 June 1994, transcript.

Kinnear, Deputy Chief David, 28 September 1992, transcript.

Knight, Firefighter Gerald, 19 June 1991, transcript.

Marcell, Firefighter Andrew, 23 September 1998, transcript.

McCormack, Sr. Deputy Chief James, 14 June 1991, transcript.

McGee, Captain Raymond, 26 October 2000, transcript.

McGrory. Deputy Chief Albert, 31 August 1991, transcript.

Miller, Battalion Chief Joseph, 16, 21 August 1991, transcript.

Redden, Fire Chief Joseph, 16 September 2002, transcript.

Rosamilia, Captain John, in discussion with the author, 19 August 2004.

Ryan, Battalion Chief John, in discussion with the author, 18 August 2004.

Smith, Firefighter James, 2 September 1998, transcript.

Stoffers, Battalion Chief Carl, 2 September 1998, transcript.

Vesey, Firefighter Edward, 15 June 1999, transcript.

Vetrini, Captain Joseph, 14 September 1993, transcript.

Wall, Deputy Chief Edward, 13 September 2000, transcript.

Wargo, Captain Andrew, 6 June 1991, transcript.

SOURCES CONSULTED

Cunningham, John T. Newark. Newark, NJ: The New Jersey Historical Society, 1988.

Governor's Select Commission on Civil Disorder. Report for Action. Trenton: 1968.

Governor's Select Commission on Civil Disorder. Records, 1968. Trenton: New Jersey State Archives.

National Advisory Commission on Civil Disorders. Report of the National Advisory Commission on Civil Disorders. Washington, D.C.: Government Printing Office, 1968; reprint, New York: Bantam Books, 1968.

Newark Fire Department. Annual Reports 1966 –2002.

Newark Fire Department. Company Journals – July 1967 Engine Companies 6, 9, 10, 14,19, 27. Truck Companies 1, 3, 4, 6, 10. Salvage Company 1. Fireboat 1.

Newark Fire Department. Notice No. 81 – July 24, 1967.

New Jersey State Patrolmen's Benevolent Association. The Road to Anarchy: Findings of the Riot Study Commission of the New Jersey PBA, 1968.

Porambo, Ron. No Cause for Indictment: An Autopsy of Newark. New York: Holt, Reinhart and Winston, 1971.

Redden, Joseph. Notes on Riots given to Battalion Chief Edward Wall for Congressional Testimony. Unpublished, 1967.

U.S. News and World Report, March of the News: "Newark Race Riots: (Open Rebellion- Just Like War)." 24 July 1967, p. 6 and p. 8.

Winters, Stanley B. From Riot to Recovery: Newark Ten Years After. Washington, D.C.: University Press of America, 1979.

Alarm Signals of the Newark Fire Department

Appendix A consists of information I garnered from Newark Fire Department company journals of July, 1967. Only twelve of the forty-one journals could be located by 2004. Fortunately, these were from companies scattered around the city and so give a fairly complete picture. Of the 364 responses made by the NFD, 328 are recorded in these books. Under normal circumstances, all of these responses should have been recorded between these journals, but the circumstances those four nights were not ordinary.

The most compelling reading of these journals is from Six Engine on Springfield Avenue and Hunterdon Street. The concise, terse writing captures the intense drama of those four nights of madness.

What is included in this appendix is taken verbatim from these books. This is how the firefighters in Newark's firehouses recorded what was happening around them.

For many readers, the information contained here will be foreign. Hopefully, the following quick explanation will make the task of deciphering the material easier.

Signals were sent out over a telegraph system much as they were in the 19th century. The system consisted of street pull boxes which when activated by pulling a small handle transmitted a sequence of bells to fire dispatch which was located on the second floor of City Hall. The dispatchers would then send this signal out over the system to all the firehouses in the city as two groups of bells. Station 4219 would come over as four bells in quick succession, followed by a pause, then two bells, a pause, one bell, a pause, and finally nine bells. This would be repeated. This station corresponds to Belmont Avenue and 17th Avenue, present day Irvine Turner Boulevard and 17th Avenue, and was the station Twelve Engine responded to for the car fire at the Fourth Precinct.

Every company in the city would record this station in their journal along with the time it was received and the companies dispatched. When companies called back in service after the alarm, a return call would be sent out over the telegraph system on what was called the joker circuit. This made a clicking sound and was located in the alarm consoles, cabinets that housed the circuitry of the telegraph, which were located in the watch rooms of the firehouses. The time this signal was received would be recorded next to the original alarm along with the company that was returned to service. Obviously, companies not in quarters could not record this information in their journal. Hence, the less than perfect record obtained from these journals. At the height of the fires, there were no companies left in their quarters.

The number designations of the signals indicated how many companies were dispatched. If a full assignment was sent to a station, only the box number would be sent over the system. Four engines, two trucks, a Battalion Chief and a Deputy Chief would respond. If a reduced assignment of two engines, a truck company, and a Battalion Chief was dispatched, then a group of nine bells would be transmitted before the box number. A response of one engine, one truck, and a Battalion Chief would receive eight bells before the box number. This signal would be sent over a small bell on the alarm console. If a single unit was sent out, the small bell would be utilized with the number of the unit ringing out over the circuit. Reduced assignments, the bulk of responses over the course of these four nights, are called signal nines. These are the task forces that were recorded. If the officer on the scene of an alarm with a reduced assignment felt he needed the full assignment he would ask dispatch for a signal ten.

Radio signals coming in from the field to fire dispatch have a 300 designation in front of the bell alarm number. A 309 (three oh nine) would mean that two engines, one truck, and a Battalion Chief were held on the scene. A 308 (three oh eight) would hold one engine, one truck, and a Battalion Chief. A 305 would hold one company. A signal 300 is a malicious false alarm.

Other signals transmitted across the telegraph system include a 5-5-5 (a special message over the department radio would follow), a 2-2-2-2 (recall of all off duty personnel), 7-7 (emergency procedures are in effect), 9-9 (all alarms will have a response of a signal 9 without the nine bells preceding the box number), and 4-4-4-4 (announcing the death of firefighter).

In addition to these signals, a signal bell was sent over the system twice a day at the change of tours (8 o'clock in the morning and 6 o'clock at night). In over twenty-six years on the Newark Fire Department, I know of no time when these "time blows" were missed. The bell would be followed by an announcement of the radio station identification and frequency, the tour and chief officers on duty, and any announcements authorized by fire headquarters.

I have used military time through out this appendix. This is not how it was recorded in 1967. The standard A.M. and P.M. designation were used by the NFD at the time. The 24 hour military system is used to avoid confusion. The time recorded to the right of many of the alarms is the return call for the last company on the scene of that particular alarm.

Also included is other information from the report of the Governor's Select Commission on Civil Disorder. This is used to pinpoint events that occurred in Newark, but were not recorded in the journals of the fire department.

Alarms and Events Recorded in Company Journals*

18:00   Tour 2 *Wednesday July 12, 1967*

18:30   Signal 5 Trk 10   18:57

18:40   Station 4233   18:42
         (Avon Avenue and Bergen Street)

Engine 10 responded to Avon and Bergen. Signal 305,
Engine 18.

Engine 6 received and responded to Station 4233.
Received signal 305.

19:05   Six Engine first aid - citizen Nakomis Cathcant 345
         Springfield Avenue rendered first aid for cut on head.

19:15   Station 3523   19:17
         (Broadway and Verona Avenue)
         Signal 300

20:24   Station 4848 *(South 17ᵗʰ St. School*   20:36
         between 17ᵗʰ & 18ᵗʰ Street)

Engine 6 received and responded to Station 4848.
Received Signal 300.

21:00   Station 3125   21:02
                  (Summer and 7ᵗʰ Avenues)

21:35   Signal 5 Engine 28   22:05

22:22   Signal 5 Engine 13   22:30

22:45   Station 1131   22:48
         (13ᵗʰ Avenue and Boston Street)

---

* Journals from the following companies were used: Engines 6, 9,
10, 14, 19, and 27; Trucks 1, 3, 4, 6, 10; Salvage 1. Included are
times given in the Governor's Commission <u>Report for Action</u> for
certain events that occurred in Newark during the riots.

Signal 300 Engine 6 received and responded to Station 1131.

22:50   Station 2422   22:51
         (Frelinghuysen Avenue & Earl Street)

Engine 10 responded to Frelinghuysen Avenue and Earl Street. No cause for alarm. Signal 300

23:46   Signal 5 Engine 12   24:00 **24:00**

Midnight *Thursday July 13, 1967*

00:10   **Signal 8 Station 4219**   00:31

Fourth Precinct incident

00:14   Station 1581   00:25
         (South Orange & Monticello Avenues)
00:27 **Signal 5 Engine 6**   00:35

Assist 12 Engine at Fourth Precinct
Notified by operator to respond on a Signal 5 to 17th Avenue and Livingston Street for an auto fire. Ordered out of area by Battalion Chief Nolan after bottles and stones were thrown at apparatus and men. F/M Wiggins received laceration on neck. Rear tail light broken and roof of cab dented.

00:31   Signal 5 Engine 2   00:35

00:40 **5-5-5 Special message from 1st Deputy Chief. All members responding to the 1st Deputy Division are to wear helmets.**

01:11   Station 1146
         (Boyden and James Streets)   Signal 300

01:20   Station 5411   01:23
         (New Jersey RR Ave. & Chestnut St.) Signal 300

02:28   Signal 5 Engine 20   02:39
07:26   Signal 5 Engine 12   07:48

07:45   Station 4748   07:57
(Hayes Homes 17th Avenue Op. Livingston St.)

Engine 10 responded on cover for Engine 12.

Engine 6 responded to #7 17th Avenue, 12 story brick apartments. Clogged incinerator 12th floor. Cleared same and ventilated.   Signal 308

08:00   Tour 4 *Thursday July 13, 1967*

08:59   Signal 5 Salvage 1   09:35

09:10   Signal 5 Truck 2   10:41

09:19   Signal 5 Truck 9   10:22

09:55   Station 4233   10:37
           (Avon Avenue and Bergen Street) Signal 309

Engine 10 responded, ordered by Acting Deputy Chief Grehl to search and ventilate upper floors due to cellar fire at 184 Avon Avenue a three story frame dwelling. Later ordered into cellar to assist other companies. Ordered to quarters by same officer.

Engine 6 responded to a cellar fire at Avon and Bergen. Stretched two lengths 2 ½" feeder, supplied by Engine 12. Stretched and operated
four lengths of 1 ½" pre-connected in cellar. Ordered up by Battalion Chief 4. Pump time 20 minutes. Used four masks at 10 minutes each.

10:05   Signal 5 Engine 5   12:21

10:47   Station 2343   10:54
           (Broad and Camp Streets)   Signal 300

Engine 10 notified by operator to respond to 21 Camp Street. After investigating found no cause.

11:00   Station 3154   12:26
           (Crane and Wood Streets)

Engine 9 notified by operator to respond to 3 Wood Street. Received Station 3154, fire located on fourth floor at 3 Wood Street. Stretched 1 ½" line four lengths to fire, 1 line 2 ½" five lengths feeder line from hydrant at corner of Crane and Wood Street. Tenant Pedro Ruicurn, apartment 22. Owner Raymond Marzulli, 850 Broad Street, Newark, Engine duty 2 hours.

Salvage 1 responded to 3 Wood Street, fire fourth floor, spread 3 covers, 1 water chute, secured, left two plastic covers and 1 water chute, apartment #16.

| 11:25 | Signal 5 Engine 27 | 11:44 |

Responded on report by a citizen of an accident at railroad bridge. Truck owned by Sam Bendri & Son, 867 Washington (?) Lic # 149-061, driver Gene Nynan. Notified Police, stood by until arrival of radio police, returned to quarters.

| 12:16 | Station 4323 | 12:26 |
| | *(South 10th and Blum Streets)* Signal 305 | |

Engine 6 responded and ordered up at scene.

12:46	Signal 5 Engine 16	14:20
13:01	Signal 8 Station 4726	13:13
	(Scudder Homes)	

13:40   Engine 6 notified the operator to send Emergency Squad to 345 Springfield Avenue, third floor, for injured citizen.

13:47	Signal 5 BC 5	14:39
15:57	Station 4846	16:16
	(Avon Avenue School)	

Engine 6 responded. Ordered up at scene.
Signal 305

16:33	Station 2326	16:55
	(Pennsylvania and Sherman Avenues)	
	Signal 308	

Truck 1 responded to 54 Pennsylvania Ave. Fire in Hallway, ventilated and overhauled.

Engine 10 responded, found fire in papers and rags in front of rear first floor apartment of 54 Pennsylvania Avenue. Fire spread to door and door frame. Used 1 booster 15 minutes – owner Mrs. Grace Short, tenant Fred Lopez sounded Signal 100. Headquarters 5 is investigating.

16:48   Signal 5 Engine 12   16:58

17:27   Signal 8 Station 4733   17:38
(Wright Homes, Montgomery and Prince Streets)

18:00   Tour 2 *Thursday July 13, 1967*

18:05   Director Caufield and Fire Chief Redden in 6 Engine's quarters.

19:00   Signal 5 Engine 29   19:04

19:01   Battalion Chief Hug in Engine 10's quarters, read new operating procedures in case of riots.

19:40   **Truck 3 All loose equipment on apparatus put into compartments as ordered by Chief Engineer.**

19:45   Signal 9 Station 3141   19:49
        (Clifton and Park Avenues)   Signal 305

Engine 9 responded on a Signal 9 Station 3141, automobile opposite 173 Clifton Avenue. Fire in carburator out on arrival. Owner and driver Acie L. Early, 291 Bergen Street, Newark,1966 Buick. Out 14 minutes.

20:12   Signal 9 Station 4219   20:24
        (Seventeenth Avenue and Livingston Street)

Engine 6 responded to Signal 9 Station 4219, fire involving Volkswagon auto on 17th Avenue between Lillie and Livingston Streets. Used one booster ten minutes.

20:15   Battalion Chief Tangedi briefed men in responding as task forces from 18:00 to 0800 until further notice.

> 20:20   Signal 9 Station 4261   20:27
> *(Bergen Street and West Runyon)*

> 20:23   Signal 5 Engine 27   20:38

Responded to signal 5 to Avenue I under South Street ramp used 2 booster lines. Engine duty 10. Out 15.

> 20:24   Truck 4 – B.C. Zieser visited quarters and instructed company on procedures for civil disorders.

> 20:32   Signal 9 Station 4324   20:39
> *(Rose and Brenner Sts.)*

Engine 6 received and responded to Station 4324.

> 20:35   Signal 5 Engine 6   20:39

On the way to Rose and Brenner Streets found fire in storefront at 425 Springfield Avenue, a four story brick. Used one booster, five minutes.

> 20:37   Signal 8 Station 5251   20:40
> *(NJ Railroad Avenue and Walnut Street)*
> Signal 300

> 20:42   Signal 9 Station 4219   20:45
> *(17th Avenue and Livingston Street)* Signal 305

Engine 6 received and responded to Station 4219, Signal 9, auto fire on 17th Avenue and Boyd Street. Unable to respond in 17th Avenue due to stoning. Returned to quarters.

> 20:45   Signal 5 Engine 32   20:57

21:00   *(Looting becomes intense on Springfield Avenue)*

> 21:15   Signal 5 Engine 19   21:37

Engine 19 notified by operator to respond to Routes 22 and 1. Auto fire – 1961 Chevrolet 2 door sedan. License LXW-532. Owner Jose Cuerto, 138 Sherman Avenue, Newark – fire in ignition wires and floor mat, used co2 and booster. Requested Special Service deliver CO2.

21:17   Signal 9 Station 1368   21:18
         (Dickerson Street and 5th   Street) Signal 300

21:18   Signal 9 Station 4118   21:19
         (Montgomery and Prince Sts.)   Signal 300
21:20 Battalion Chief M. Tangridi entered quarters of Truck 6 and by written order of Chief of Department J. Redden instructed men on duty as to procedures to be taken during these uncertain times.

21:27   Signal 9 Station 4118   21:28
         (Montgomery and Prince Sts.)   Signal 300

21:29   Signal 9 Station 4186   21:43
         (Mercer Street and Howard Street)

Engine 6 received and responded to Station 4186. Fire in three story frame at Howard between Springfield and Mercer Street. Assisted Engine 20.

21:52   Signal 9 Station 4214   21:57
(Springfield Avenue and Sayre Street)
 Signal 300
Engine 6 received and responded to Signal 9 Station 4214, Signal 300. Shut off hydrant on corner of Springfield Avenue and Sayre Street. Received and responded via radio to Springfield and Bergen Street. Molotov Cocktail, extinguished same.

22:03   Signal 9 Station 4218 Task Force #1   00:06 *(Springfield and Morris)*

Engine 6 spotted gang throwing Molotov cocktail into Flax's Baby Store on the corner of Springfield Avenue and Morris Avenue. Ordered Station 4218 to be sent in via radio. Responded. Engine took green top hydrant north west corner Morris Avenue and Springfield Avenue. Stretched one line 2 ½" three lengths to store and operated into same. Stretched one line 2 ½" three lengths and also operated same into store. Reduced line to one line 1 ½" three lengths and operated on second and third floors. Supplied one line 2 ½" for Engine 18. Also supplied one line 1 ½" four lengths to another company. A task force three was sounded for this station. Used four masks fifteen minutes each. Engine duty ninety minutes. Fireman Charpentier received laceration on left index finger. Battalion Chief Nolan injured his back when he fell in the street

Truck 3 Signal 9 Station 4218. Responded to Springfield and Morris. Working fire in 3 story frame on Southeast corner. Used hooks, axes, haligan tools, also overhauled. Company duty 35 minutes. Ordered up by Chief Nolan.

Salvage 1 responded to Station 4218, Springfield and Morris Avenues. Ventilated, used 2 ½" line.

| 22:03 | Signal 5 Truck 1 | 23:15 |

Special called to 346 Springfield Avenue, Flax Department Store, 3 story brick, raised Snorkel – hooks and axes – ventilated and overhauled, ordered up by Chief Redden.

| 22:04 | Signal 9 Station 4218 Task Force 2 | 00:02 |

| 22:05 | Signal 9 Station 4218 Task Force 3 | 23:39 |

Engine 10 responded on Station 4218 to Springfield and Morris Avenues. Ordered to stand-by by Battalion Chief Nolan, assisted in stretching lines. Ordered to Quarters by Chief Redden.

| 22:12 | Signal 9 Station 4124 | 22:13 |
| | *(Springfield Avenue and William Street)* | Signal 300 |

| 22:18 | Signal 5 Engine 11 | 23:45 |

Engine 11 in Engine 6's quarters as Engine 6.

| 22:26 | Signal 5 Engine 6 | 22:29 |

Engine 11 responded as Engine 6 on Signal 5's to Springfield Avenue and Sayre Street, Springfield Avenue and Fairmont Avenue, and 114 16th Avenue. All signal 300's.

22:33	Signal 9 Station 4348	22:36
	(16th Avenue and South 7th Street)	

Salvage 1 responded on the air from Station 4218 to a signal 9 Station 4348. Damage to apparatus on Springfield Avenue to right cover door by rocks. Signal 300

22:41   Signal 5 Engine 14

22:45	Signal 9 Station 4226	22:50
	(18th Avenue and Fairview Avenue) Signal 300	

Responded to Signal 9 Station 4226.

22:59   Signal 5 Engine 6   23:18

Signal 5 Springfield and Fairmont Avenues. Good Humor truck, used booster 15/60.

First Aid – Engine 11 as Engine 6 rendered first aid to Faik Yar of 76 Grant Street, was removed in private car to City Hospital.

23:38   Signal 5 Engine 6   00:17

Engine 11 returned to their quarters.

23:42	Signal 9 Station 4117	23:42
	(Morton Street and Prince Street) Signal 300	

23:47	Signal 9 Station 4118	23:49
	(Montgomery Street and Prince Street) Signal 300	

23:52	Signal 9 Station 1227 Task Force 1	00:53
	(Morris Avenue and Cabinet Street)	

Truck 3 Station 1227 responded to working fire at 56-58-60 Hunterdon Street, three 3-story frames. Used ladder pipe and worked all buildings. Stretched 10 lengths of 2

½" hose from Engine 10 as feed. Used hooks, axes, one 30' ladder, one 10' ladder. Overhauled, used one line 1 ½" 3 lengths into 60 Hunterdon on all floors and worked.

23:54   Signal 9 Station 1227   Task Force 2

23:55   Signal 9 Station 1227   Task Force 3   00:23

23:59   Signal 9 Station 7221   00:06
         (396 Littleton Ave.)   Signal 300

23:59   Signal 5 Engine 10   00:25

24:00   Midnight   *Friday July 14, 1967*

00:01   Signal 5 Engine 10   01:05

Engine 10 notified by operator to respond to Hunterdon Street fire (Station 1227), three buildings fully involved. Stretched two lines of 2 1/2" supply, one to Truck 7 for ladder pipe eight lengths, one to register 19 supply. Took one line 1 ½" 5 lengths to third floor. Engine duty 90 minutes. Mask 2 @ 15 minutes.

00:14   Signal 9 Station 2112   00:38
         (Market Street and Halsey Street)

Truck 1, 164 Market Street, no cause, used Snorkel.

00:19   Signal 9 Station 4353   00:22
(Springfield and Littleton Avenues)   Signal 305

Received and responded to Station 4353, fire in litter basket. Unable to extinguish due to stoning. Returned to quarters.

00:20   Signal 8 Station 2326   00:23
         (Pennsylvania and Sherman Avenues)   Signal 300

00:24   Signal 5 Engine 12

00:25   Engine 12 relocated in quarters of Engine Ten.

00:30   Signal 9 Station 4118   00:37

(Montgomery Street and Prince Street)

Engine 6 received and responded to Station 4118, fire in
three story frame Prince and Morton Streets.
Used booster five minutes. A signal 9 for this station.

Salvage 1 responded on the air from Station 7221 to
Prince and Montgomery Streets, worked.

00:33   Signal 9 Station 1128   01:04
         (South Orange Avenue and Prince Street)

00:35   Signal 9 Station 4141 Task Force 1   00:56
         (Spruce Street and Carlton Avenue)

00:36   Signal 9 Station 4141 Task Force 2

Engine 27 Unit 2 responded to Charlton and Spruce,
found fire in one story brick building, used two 2 ½" lines
4 lengths each. Used 3 masks 20 minutes each. Ordered
up by Chief Redden. While returning to quarters ordered
to report to Station 1394.

Truck 4 responded to 18th Avenue and Prince Street,
01:30 found fire in one story non-fire resistant shoe store,
used hooks, axes, and assisted. (Booked as 4118)

Engine 19 responded on Task Force 2 to Station 4141,
Spruce and Charlton Streets – While enroute was
involved in an accident with Wagon Register 32,
(F/M Suehodalski) driving and Olds 88 License # LSC-
574. Three passengers in auto removed to City Hospital
in City ambulance – further information not available at
this time. Register 32 taken to city garage at Empire
Street by city wrecker. Company returned to quarters
riding one piece. 1 officer and 3 men, Elizabeth Fire
Department apparatus and Battalion Chief in quarters.

00:38   Signal 9 Station 4311   00:49
         (15th Avenue and Camden Street)

Engine 6 received via radio and responded to Station
4311, Signal 9. Fire in store at 362 15th Avenue. Used
one booster ten minutes.

00:47   Signal 5 Engine 16

00:48   Signal 5 Engine 28

00:50   Signal 5 Engine 21

00:52   Truck 7 in quarters of Truck 3 to ride as truck 3,
1 officer and 3 men.

00:55   Signal 9 Station 4225   01:03
        (18th Avenue and Bergen Street)
Engine 6 received and responded to Station 4225, fire in
panel truck, corner 18th Avenue and Bergen Street. Used
booster ten minutes.

00:56   Signal 9 Station 2418   01:00
        (Sherman Avenue and Miller Street)   Signal 300

00:57   Signal 5 Engine 7

01:00   Engine 16 relocated in quarters of Engine 10.

01:00 – 01:30   Members of Engine 27 report on recall.

01:02   Signal 9 Station 1343   01:03
        (South Orange Avenue and Bergen Street) Signal 300

01:04   Signal 5 Engine 5

01:08   Signal 9 Station 2212   13:38
        (Broad Street and Edison Place)

Task Force 1 Truck 1 Station 2212. Fire in 805 Broad
Street. Responded, raised Snorkel. Fire four story
wooden frame building. 3 Stores on 1st floor. Used
deluge set , removed cornices, walls, ceilings, ect,
overhauled. Raised 25', 30', 14' ladders. Tour 4 relived
Tour 2 and recall men. At above alarm F/M Farrell
injured right elbow, F/M Merenghi injured left hand.
Both remained on duty. Returned 13:38, out 12 hours 30
minutes.

Salvage 1 responded on the air to Broad and Bradford Place, used smoke ejector, operated lines, and ventilated. E & J: 50. Mask: 90. Porta-lite lost on ground floor under debris. F/M Alfano injuryed by falling wall in backdraft. Injured back and scrotum (balls). F/M Parisi suffered chest pains and received oxygen.

Engine 10 responded to 807-813 Broad Street, three story brick fully involved, stretched 1 ½" line four lengths to first floor, ordered out of building. 2 lines of 2 ½" supply 6 lengths then operated deck pipe. Pump time. Mask time four at thirty minutes.Tour 4 relieved Tour 2 at this fire and overhauled. Stretched 14 lengths 2 ½" and 9 1 ½" for two lines. Engine duty 2 x 12 hours = 24 hours. Out of service 13 hours and 10 minutes. Received 40 gallons of fuel at this fire.

Engine 6 responded to a working   12:04 fire at 809-11-13 Broad Street. Straight stretched three lengths 2 ½" feeder from high pressure hydrant at #15 Bradford Place to south end of fire building. Stretched two 2 ½" lines two lengths each and supplied ladderpipe of Truck Company #1. Stretched two 2 ½" handlines four lengths each and operated in rear of buildings. Later ordered to operate deluge set in rear. Complied. Tour #2 relieved by Tour #4 at fire. Ordered up by Battalion Chief Iannuzi.

01:11   Signal 9 Station 1349   Task Force 1
        (South Orange Avenue and Camden Street)

Truck 10 Received signal 9 Station 1349, responded to 205 Bergen Street. Ordered by Chief Nolan to stretch 1 line 2 ½" hose from Engine 20 to rear yard of 205 Bergen street, two 4-story brick buildings involved in fire. While responding, men and apparatus were hit with bottles and rocks, right and left windshields broken by bottles, both driver and Captain were showered with glass in face and eyes, remained on duty. F/M Tully received first aid for eyes from Rescue Squad.

Engine 27 Unit 2 responded to South Orange Avenue and Camden Street. Reported to B.C. Zieser, ordered to work.

Stretched one line of 2 ½" 14 lengths to third floor at 210 Camden to work on fire at 208 Camden. Used 2 masks @ 20 minutes. Later ordered up by B.C. Zieser. Ordered to report to Engine company 6 quarters and ride as Engine 6.

01:15   Signal 9 Station 2212   Task Force 2   13:37

01:19   Signal 9 Station 2212   Task Force 3   09:33

Engine 9 responded on third task force to Signal 9 Station 2212. Stretched one line 1 ½" hose four lengths to second floor of three story brick at 807 Broad Street. Ordered out of building by Chief in charge. Used deck pipe on Register 65, three feed lines. Two from high pressure hydrant southwest corner of Broad and Market Streets. One line from Engine 10, 15 lengths 2 ½" hose used. Four masks used two hours. Engine duty eight hours. Register 43 with one man F/M Raffa ordered to quarters of Engine 1. F/M Raffa cut palm of right hand at Station 2122. Tour 4 relieved Tour 2 at 0800. Roll call 1 officer and three men. F/M Skinner and F/M Baddoto Tour 3 volunteered to work with Tour 4.

01:24   Signal 5 Engine 29

01:25   Signal 9 Station 1349   Task Force 2

01:30   2-2-2-2 Re-Call

01:30   **7-7 Emergency Procedures in Effect**

01:35   Truck 1 members begin to report on recall.

01:38   Signal 5 Engine 17   01:56

01:39   Truck 6 received orders over the radio from Chief Redden to call all available men.

01:45   Elizabeth Fire Department Engine 9, one Captain and three men, Acting Battalion Chief Conkler and Aide in Engine 19 quarters, in service at 0205 with Newark Fire Department escort, F/M Minatee.

01:53   Signal 5 Engine 2   01:56

01:54   Signal 5 Engine 4

01:55   Signal 5 Engine 29

02:05   Men begin to report to Truck 6 on recall.

02:07   Signal 5 Engine 12   02:15

02:11   Two Captains report to Truck 6 on recall.

02:12   Signal 5 Engine 2

02:13   Signal 5 Engine 4

02:15   Members of Engine 10 begin to report in quarters on recall.

02:19   Signal 9 Station 4342   07:10
         (Clinton Avenue and Osborne Terrace)
         02:20   **National Guard and State Police requested**

    02:22   Signal 9 Station 4214
         (Springfield Avenue and Sayre Street)

    02:23   Signal 9 Station 1222
         (12th Avenue and Hunterdon Street)

    02:26   Signal 9 Station 4232   06:46
         (Avon Avenue and Badger Avenue)
Truck 4 responded to Avon and Badger, found fire in one story non-fire resistant shed and garage. Worked in conjunction with Engine 9, Elizabeth FD. Ordered to quarters by East Orange Battalion Chief.   While returning to quarters, ordered to Bergen Street and 15th Avenue.

Elizabeth Fire Department   03:25
responded to fire at 100 Jeliff, Used 12 lengths 2 ½" and 6 lengths 1 ½" hose. Captain Ed Dunn Engine 12 rode with Elizabeth Fire Department.

    02:30   Fireman Prachar in Engine Ten's quarters on
         recall.

    02:31   Signal 5 Truck 11

    02:31   Signal 9 Station 4311
         (15th Avenue and Camden Street)

Truck 7 as Truck 3, company responded on Signal 9 Station 4311. Overhauled store located at Bergen and 15th Avenue. Ordered up by Captain and returned to

60

Truck 3 quarters. (Engine 17 relocated to Engine 7 quarters.)

Truck 4 reported to B.C. Caufield, used hooks, axes, and ladders. The following members participated: Chief Schmidt, Captain Suzzolino, F/M B. Swider, D. Kraemer, A. Retorta, J. Salonowski, Fieney.

02:35	Signal 5 Truck 5	02:55
02:38	Signal 5 Engine 28	02:55
02:38	Signal 5 Truck 12	02:55
02:59	Signal 9 Station 2229 *(Walnut Street and Orchard Street)*	

While in service as Engine 2 Register 43 of Engine 9 responded to Burke (Towers?) Walnut and Orchard Streets. Used two lines 1 ½" three and 2 lengths. Engine Duty one hour. As Engine 10 responded to alarms at Bergen and Rose Streets – Springfield and Morris Avenues – 15th Avenue and 12th Street – Washington and Crawford Streets. Used booster on last location, building on southwest corner, two story brick.

03:06   Captain Ed Dunn in Engine 19's quarters to ride with Elizabeth Fire Department.

03:07   Engine 13 relocated in Engine 10's quarters as Engine 10. The following companies are out of service: Engines 1, 2, 4, 5, 6, 9, 11, 12, 13, 14, 15, 16, 17, 18, 20, 21, 26, 32.

03:17   Signal 5 Engine 8

03:20   Signal 5 Engine 7

03:30   Signal 9 Station 2424
         (Elizabeth Avenue and East Alpine Street)

Engine 13 responded as Engine 10 to 123 Elizabeth Avenue. Rubbish in front of Motor Club of America offices. Engine duty 5 minutes.

Engine 19 responded on Station 2424, Signal 9
         Engine 10 reported Signal 305.

Salvage 1 responded on the air to numerous runs during the night which are unaccounted for, but we did not work at them.

03:32　　Signal 9 Station 4114　　　　　　　　　05:50
　　　　(Springfield Avenue and Belmont Avenue)
Truck 6 responded to Springfield and Beacon Street. Upon arrival reported to 4th Battalion Chief James T. Nolan. He ordered them to proceed to Waverly Avenue near Broome Street. Responded and found a working fire on Waverly Avenue. Used 20' and 24' foot ladders. Later ordered to go in service as Truck 1. On route to Truck 1's quarters received radio alarm and responded to 211 Miller Street and assisted Elizabeth FD with fire first floor of a fruit and vegetable storage. Later ordered to the Eight Cucolini Brothers Furniture 37 Broadway. Reported to Chief of Department Joseph M. Redden and ordered to raise aerial to roof of building, a working fire, opened up roof and later operated inside on second floor pulling ceilings. Later returned to quarters and notified operator that 1 Acme Mask Harness was stolen from apparatus, 1 Captain's hand held light was missing from Waverly Avenue fire. 1 six foot pike pole broken at 37 Broadway. (Used two Scott tanks.) Returned 0550.

03:35　　Signal 9 Station 2239　　　　　　　　　03:46
　　　　(McCarter Highway and Edison Place)

Truck 3 responded to 772 McCarter Highway. Found fire in one story brick, used hooks and axes.

03:38　　Signal 9 Station 4139
　　　　(Waverly Avenue opposite Avon Place)

03:50　　Signal 5 Engine 19　　　　　　　　　　04:20

Engine 19 responded to Turnpike truck fire North Bound at Exit 15 – overheated brakes. Pennisula Equipment Company, Daysboro, Delaware. Driver Lee Lynch Frankfort, Delaware Driver License C-42-365. Used booster 15 minutes. Notified shop Engine 19 Register 96 needs battery. Mechanic reported in quarters.

03:55   Signal 9   Station 4161
           (Rose Street and Barclay Street)   Signal 300

      04:03   Signal 9 Station 4117
              (Morton Street and Prince Street)

      04:12   Signal 9 Station 5576
              (Avenue A and Miller Street)

      04:14   Signal 8 Station 4247
              (Bergen Street and Rose Street)   Signal 305

04:15   Register 40 in Engine 27's quarters with make up company. Acting Captain F/M Theiss, F/M Lopes, F/M Paradiso, F/M Greeley.

      Engine 9 in Engine 10's quarters as Engine 10.

      04:28   Signal 8 Station 4247
              (Bergen Street and Rose Street) - Signal 305

      04:34   Signal 5   Engine 4

      04:34   Signal 5   Engine 2

      04:26   Signal 5   Engine 18

      04:43   Signal 9 Station 4218   05:00
              (Springfield Avenue and Morris Avenue)

      Truck 3 responded to 394 Morris Avenue, used hooks and axes. Signal 308

      04:47   Signal 5   Engine 2

      04:58   Signal 9 Station 4465   05:08
              (15th Avenue and 17th Street)   Signal 305

      Elizabeth Fire Company in charge of Captain Buba 1 – 3, Battalion Chief car acting B/C Kunka and driver.

      05:04   Signal 5   Engine 29   05:11

      05:07   Signal 9 Station 4456   05:12
              (15th Avenue and 12th Street)   Signal 300

05:20   Engine 27 reported in quarters to ride as
Engine Company 6, one officer and three men on orders
from department operator. Engine 27 Unit 1 reported to
Engine Company 1's quarters on orders of operator.

Engine 18

05:30   *102 State Police Officers arrive in the city, National Guard*
follow later

05:36   Signal 5 Engine 19   06:05

Responded on a Signal five to truck fire at Loading dock
Allstate Air Cargo 35 Fenwick Street. Ford van License
number X29718. Fire in double right tires and wood floor
of truck, used booster and three lengths 1 ½" from high
pressure hydrant.
Notified by quarters Elizabeth Fire Department to return
to Elizabeth, left quarters at 06:15.

05:41   Signal 5 Engine 6

Engine 27, Unit 2 responded as Six Engine to 226
Springfield Avenue. Found rubbish in the street. Used
one booster line. Engine duty 10 minutes. Out 20
minutes.

05:49   Signal 5 BC 3

05:50   An officer has been shot – all (O negative
blood donors are hereby notified to donate blood. Blood
type is O positive.

05:53   Signal 9 Station 2338   06:14
         (Washington and Crawford Streets   Signal 305

06:10   Signal 9 Station 2134   06:20
         (Broad Street and Central Avenue)

06:15   Signal 5 Engine 18

06:30   Spare unit #42 in 10 Engine's quarters as

Engine 10. Roll call 1 officer and 7 men, all on recall, all members on Engine 10.

06:40	Signal 9 Station 4185	06:55
	(Court Street and Carlton Street)	

Engine 27 received and responded as Engine 6 to Station 4185, Prince and Court Streets. Found small fire at Prince and Court, used one booster line. Engine duty five minutes, out ten minutes.
Fireman Feeley Engine 6 Tour 1 riding with Engine 27 since 0230.

06:47	Signal 8 Station 7161	06:55
	(800 Broad Street)	

06:55	Signal 9 Station 4639	06:59
	(Custer Avenue and Chadwick Avenue)	
	Signal 300	

07:00	Signal 9 Station 2424	07:10
	(Elizabeth Avenue and East Alpine Street) Signal 300	

07:07	Signal 9 Station 4455	07:12
	(16th Avenue and 13th Street) Signal 300	

Engine 27 as Engine 6 received and responded to Signal 9 Station 4455, 16th Avenue and 13th Street. Signal 300.

07:19	Signal 5 Engine 14	07:24
07:20	Signal 5 Engine 6	
07:33	Signal 5 Truck 5	09:08
07:41	Signal 5 Engine 2	08:00
07:42	Signal 5 Battalion 2	
07:43	Signal 5 Engine 15	
07:43	Signal 5 Engine 7	09:50
07:44	Signal 5 Engine 8	12:01
07:58	Signal 9 Station 1227	07:59
	(Morris Avenue and Cabinet Street) Signal 300	

08:00 **Tour 4** *Friday July 14, 1967*

08:02 **All Chiefs to Hdqts**

08:16   Signal 9 Station 1349   08:19
              (South Orange Avenue and Camden Street)
Sig 305

08:22   Signal 9 Station 4343   08:29
              (Clinton and Chadwick Avenues)

08:29   Signal 5 BC 4   08:40

08:29   Signal 5 Engine 10   14:15

Responded to relieve Tour 2 at Broad Street fire.

08:43   Signal 5 Salvage 1

Responded to Broad Street and Bradford Place. Spread 15
plastic covers, 1 stock cover, used 2 lights, portable
generator, portable pump.

09:00   Captain Calwell of Engine 19 notified headquarters of
              accident at High and Spruce Streets – three persons taken
              to hospital.

              09:09   Signal 5 Engine 18   10:02
09:34   *Emergency Proclaimation 23:00 – 06:00 curfew, 22:00-06:00*
              Vehicle restriction

09:40   Signal 9 Station 3228   09:43
              (Broadway and Oriental Street)   Signal 300

Engine 9 received and responded on a Signal 9 Station
3228, Signal 300. Engines out: 6, 7, 8, 10, 16, 17, 18, 20.

10:16   Signal 5 Engine 18   10:19

10:26   Signal 9 Station 4455   11:35
              (16th Avenue and South 13th Street)
10:27   Signal 9 Station 4455 Task Force 2   11:07

10:32   Signal 5 Engine 14   10:40

66

Responded on Signal 5 to Camp and Broad Streets, auto fire, 1958 abandoned Plymouth sedan (no wheels, no registration) on Camp Street off Broad Street. Back seat burning. Used John Bean. Engine duty 5 minutes. Engines out of service 6, 7, 8, 10, 11, 12, 15, 16, 18, 28.

10:41   Signal 9 Station 3454   11:15
         (Springdale Avenue and North 11ᵗʰ Street)

10:44   Signal 9 Station 4245   11:52
         (Hawthorne Avenue and Bergen Street)
Truck 10 Received and responded to siganl 9 Station 4245, ordered to work, vented and overhauled. Used 2 masks 15 minutes each. Ordered up by B.C. Caufield. Out of quarters 1 hour 8 minutes. Used 85' aerial.

Salvage 1 Responded on a working fire, ordered to quarters by Battalion 1.

10:45   Engine 9's journal: Message from Chief Redden – The Newark Housing Authority has locked all doors leading to roofs of all projects in the city.

12:06   Signal 9 Station 4218   13:17
         (Springfield Avenue and Morris Avenue)

         Truck 3 received Station 4218 Signal 9. Responded to 319 Springfield Avenue. Found second floor of furniture store fully involved. Company ventilated and overhauled, raised 100' aerial and 25' ladder. 4 masks, 10 minutes each. Out of quarters 44 minutes.

Salvage 1 responded on a working fire, ordered to quarters by Battalion 1

Engine 6 responded to 319 Springfield Avenue, two story brick, Silver's Furniture Store, Owners Flax Corporation. Fire involved second floor rear. Stretched three lengths 2 ½" feeder from low pressure hydrant. Stretched two lines preconnected 1 ½", four lengths and three lengths through front window to second floor via inner staircase. Used

one 24' exterior ladder. Ordered up by Battalion Chief
Caufield. Pump time forty minutes, three masks ten
minutes.

12:08	Signal 5 Engine 5	12:20
12:30	Signal 5 Engine 4	
12:33	Signal 5 Engine 14	12:49

Received signal 5, responded to Camp and Broad Streets,
abandoned 1958 Plymouth on Camp Street No
registration. Used John Bean, engine duty 10 min.
Engines out 4, 6, 7, 8, 10, 16, 20.

12:40	Signal 5 Truck 7	
12:44	Signal 9 Station 2121	12:48
	(University Avenue and Warren Street)	
	Signal 305	

| 12:50 | Signal 5 Truck 4 | 06:15 |

Responded to 807 Broad Street, reported to D.C. Boyle
and ordered to assist with lines and overhaul. Raised one
28' ladder, used hooks and axes.
Ordered up by B.C. Griggs. Trucks out 1, 3, 7, 8, 11.

13:02	Signal 5 Engine 1	
13:12	Signal 5 Engine 7	13:15
13:17	Signal 9 Station 3212	13:23
	(Summer Avenue and Kearny Street)	

Engine 9 notified by a citizen of fire at 2 Kearny Street.
Notified operator. Received Station 3212. Cause of
alarm meat on stove apartment 23, tenant Sarah Lopez,
Owner Losu – Telephone SO2-1230.

| 13:18 | Signal 9 Station 4239 | Task Force 1 |
| | *(Clinton Avenue and Bergen Street)* | |

| 13:21 | Signal 9 Station 4239 Task Force 2 | 16:30 |

Engine 6 received Signal 9 Station 4239, responded to
working fire at 491 Clinton Avenue as Tactical Unit #2.
Stretched three lengths 2 ½" feeder,

supplied by Engine 17. Stretched one line 1 ½" pre-connected three lengths to second floor by orders of Battalion Chief Wall. Stretched and operated one line 2 ½" and operated in first floor. Ordered up by Battalion Chief Wall. Gassed up at Engine 18, took 23 gallons. Pump time 120, used three masks @ 20 minutes.

13:24	Signal 5 Engine 13	13:27
13:43	Signal 5 Engine 29	15:18
13:43	Signal 5 Truck 10	15:18

Notified by operator to respond on a signal 5 to 471-473 Clinton Avenue. Ordered to work by B.C. Wall. Assisted in wetting down and overhauling. Used 4 masks, 20 minutes each. Ordered up by B.C. Wall. Returned to quarters.

14:02	Signal 5 Battalion 3	
14:16	Signal 9 Station 4151	19:45
	(West Runyon Street and Hillside Avenue)	

Truck 1 Tour 4 relieved at Runyon and Hillside at 18:00. Used 30', 14' ladders, hooks, and axes. Out of service 5 hours. On the way back assisted in 1st aid to a female, E. Cook of 58 Richmond
Street, Newark. Called for ambulance and assisted same. Mrs. Cook said she
was thrown from a car, license plate PAG 76641.

Engine 19 received Signal 9 Station 4151 – West Runyon and Hillside – responded – fire in group of Stores – West Runyon. Stretched five lengths 2 ½" Feed line from Engine Ten at northwest corner of
West Runyon to company apparatus and five lengths of 1 ½" to roof via ladder and operated on fire – Tour 3 relieved Tour 4 at fire site – ordered up by B/C Farley and returned to quarters and service. Engine time 325 minutes.

Engine 10 responded to row of	21:31

taxpayers 44-50 West Runyon Street – corner store fully involved. Fire xtended to other stores. Used deck pipe. Register 109 to NW corner Hillside and West Runyon. Two lines, three lengths each to register 19 – also used three lengths 1 ½". Engine duty 2 x 6 hours = 12 hours. While at the scene Special Service delivered 20 gallons in register 109 – 10 gallons register 19. Tour 3 relieved Tour 4 at the scene.

14:23   Signal 9 Station 4151   Task Force 2   19:33

Truck 3 Received second alarm Station 4151. Responded to Hillside and west Runyon Street. Fire in a row of 1 story stores. Used 25', 16', deluge set, battering ram, chainsaw, hooks, and axes. Masks 120 minutes. Ordered up by Chief Farley. Fireman Serio injured right side.

Engine 14 responded to Hillside   18:31
Avenue and West Runyon Street. Operated in rear of drug store with
John Bean and four lengths of 1 ½". Three hours pump time. Two lengths of 2 ½" from Engine 19 for feed.

14:30   *Checkpoints in place*

14:32   Signal 8 Station 3458   14:43
         (Bloomfield Avenue and North 5th Street)

15:00   Signal 9 Station 4114   15:03
         (Springfield Avenue and Belmont Avenue)
15:16   Signal 8 Station 4114   15:17
         (Springfield Avenue and Belmont Avenue)

15:32   Signal 9 Station 4239   16:10
         (Clinton Avenue and Bergen Street)

15:40   Signal 9 Station 4117   15:44
         (Morton Street and Prince Street)

15:55   Signal 5 Engine 13

16:30   Signal 9 Station 2322   16:34
         (Clinton Avenue and Parkhurst Street)

70

16:33   Signal 9 Station 1338   16:35
       (12th Avenue and South 6th Street)

16:37   **Truck 10 5-5-5 By orders of B.C. Wall**
roll call at 1800 will be 1 officer (not acting) and 6 men. 1 man
to remain in quarters in reserve and 5 men to respond.

16:40   **(5-5-5) The following notice from Chief Redden. Effective at 6**
PM roll call in effect shall be – in two piece companies 2
Captains & 2 tours – each piece to ride as single companies –
one piece companies 1 Captain & 6 men – no acting officers.
Extra personnel shall be made from tour 4 to fill in with tour 3.
(Reserve units to be manned by members from one piece
units.) Extra apparatus 41 at 21 Engine – 42 at Prospect St -
43 at Prospect St – 44 at 27 – 45 at Eng 14

16:43   Signal 5 Engine 2   17:30

16:54   Signal 5 Engine 6   18:50

Signal 5, Engine 6 out of service due to exchange of
gunfire in front of quarters between snipers on roof tops
and State Police, City Police, and National Guard.
(Sniper from projects.)

16:58   Signal 5   BC 4

       Sniper from projects.

Truck 6 By orders of Battalion Chief Griggs Truck 6 will
relieve Truck 7 at fire with a roll call of one officer and
six men.

17:23   Signal 9 Station 2418   17:28
       (Sherman Avenue and Miller Street)
       Signal 300

17:40   Signal 9 Station 1216   17:45
       (South Orange Avenue and Morris Avenue)

17:41   Signal 9 Station 4733   17:50
       (Wright Homes: Montgomery Street & Prince Street)

17:49	**Recd 5-5-5 All personnel with O Negative blood gene to call headqtrs for Blood Donations (for policeman that was shot) (Request cancelled)**

17:50   Engine 19 called operator to report that crew is in quarters and asked where we are to relieve – told to stand by. Request for O positive blood for patrolman who was shot – F/M Lynch and F/M Slinhala volunteered. Notified operator of same. He will check and notify if still needed. Received radio message to effect blood donor request is cancelled.

17:52   Signal 5 Truck 8

18:00   Tour 3 *Friday July 14, 1967*
No time blow was received

18:00   Truck 6 relieved Truck 7 at Caridian   19:38
(?) Fur (?) Bedding fire on Broad St.   Overhauled, raised 35' ladder.
Company roll call one officer and six men, F/M LaTorre & Biscan remained on duty from tour 4.

Engine 27 roll call – two officers and eight men riding as two separate pieces as per emergency plan.

Engine 19 roll call – one officer and six men, two men from Fourth Tour, held F/M Scalera and F/M Highsmith. Following companies out of service: Engines 2, 4, 5, 6, 7, 10, 12, 14, 18, 20, 29, Truck 7. Transported to above fire by Engine 13.

Firemen Murry and Carragher left Engine 6's quarters with Director Caufield to give blood at Saint Michael's to a wounded patrolman.

18:16   Signal 5 Engine 2

18:25   Signal 9, Station 1412
(Central Avenue and 8th South Street)

Salvage 1 responded to 520 Central Avenue,
              Conducted search.

18:32   Signal 9, Station 4522

(Bergen Street and Renner Avenue)   Signal 300

18:38   Signal 9, Station 4117 Task Force 1   20:33
        (Morton and Prince Streets)

Engine 14 responded to Morton and Prince Streets. Fire
located in 95 Prince Street. Used two 1 ½" lines and John
Bean, three masks @ 10 minutes each. Pump time 1 hour
20 minutes. Men of tour three and four worked under
hazardous conditions. Bullets hit building above their
heads and second floor windows. Mask lost at this fire.
Engines 2, 4, 5, 10, 12, 17, 18, 19, 29 out of service.

18:47   Signal 9, Station 4117 Task Force 2   20:31

Engine 27 responded to 83 Prince Street, northwest corner
of Court Street. Operated deck pipe on three story brick
building. Later shut down and operated one 2 ½" line,
two lengths. Engine duty 1 ¼ hours.

Truck 4 responded to Court and   00:46
Prince Streets. Found four story brick fully involved.
Raised 85' aerial and placed ladder pipe to work.
Assisted with hand lines, overhauled. Ordered up by B.C.
McCormack and returned to quarters.

18:50   Signal 9, Station 4117   Task Force 3

18:52   Signal 9, Station 4117   Task Force 4   2010

Engine 9 Register 65 responded to Signal 9 Station 4117.
Took low pressure hydrant Court and Broome Streets,
stretched two lines to Court and Prince Streets into deluge
set. Ordered up by Deputy Chief Donlon. Engine duty
70 minutes.

18:59   Signal 9, Station 1216
        (South Orange Avenue and Morris Avenue)

Engine 6 responded on Signal 9 to 314 Morris Avenue,
three story frame. Fire out on arrival. Meat on stove.

19:01   Signal 5 Engine 29

19:03   Signal 5 Engine 6

Responded to 399 Hunterdon Street. Rubbishin rear vacant lot. Used one booster.   Engines 2, 4, 5, 10, 11, 12, 15, 18, 20, 29 out of service.

19:06   Signal 9, Station 1356   19:10
          (Dickerson Street and 2nd Street)

19:26   Signal 9 Station 1349   19:56
          (South Orange Avenue & Camden Street)

Engine 6 responded on a Signal 9 Station 1349 to   rubbish fire on third floor of three story non fire resistant abandoned and vacant factory type building. Used one booster fifteen minutes. Owner unknown. Engines 2, 4, 5, 10, 12, 14, 18, 29 out of service. Signal 305.

19:27   Signal 9 Station 4186   20:20
          (Mercer Street and Howard Street)

19:40   Signal 9, Station 1212   20:11
          (14th Avenue and Hayes Street)
          Signal 305

19:51   Signal 5 Truck 1   23:01

Responded on a Signal 5 to Broad and Bradford to assist Engine 2 in extinguishing small fires, used 85' Snorkel hooks and axes. Out of service 3 hours 10 minutes.

20:05   Signal 5 Engine 17   Fire in basement.

20:07   Signal 9 Station 4212   20:19
          (Springfield Avenue and Hunterdon Street)

Engine 6 responded to 297 Hunterdon Street. Rubbish in vacant apartment. Owner unknown. Used booster ten minutes. Engine Companies 2, 4, 5, 10, 12, 14, 17, 18, 19, 29 out of service.

20:10   Signal 9 Station 4522   20:42
          (Bergen Street and Renner Avenue)

74

Truck 10 Received signal 9 Station 4522. Responded to 921 Bergen Street, 3 story frame. Found fire in clothing store.

Raised one 24' and one 20' ladder. Stretched 1 line 1 ½" hose, 4 lengths. Used hooks, axes, and halligan tool. Ordered up by B.C. Kinnear. Out of quarters 38 minutes.

Engine 19 responded on cover – found fire in first floor used goods store at 921-3 Bergen Street. Occupant Silverman – three story frame building owner Mr. Kaufman – City – 4 lengths 1½" hose booster. Engine time 25 minutes. Opened floor molding second floor apartment. In quarters, in service, following companies out: Engine 2, 5, 10, 17, 18, 29.

20:33   Signal 5 Engine 6   20:44

Engine 6 responded to 295 Hunterdon Street, four story non-fire resistant vacant and abandoned building. Rubbish fire in cellar. Used one booster five minutes. Engine Companies 2, 4, 5, 10, 17, 18, 29 out of service. Found one Molotov cocktail at this fire.

20:50   Signal 9 Station 4231   21:00
         (Rose Street and Livingston Street)

Engine 6 responded to Rose and Livingston. Civilian shot. Removed victim in Salvage 2. Ordered back to quarters. Engine Companies 2, 5, 10, 12, 17, 18, 20 out of service.

20:55   Signal 9 Station 4833   21:33
         (Montgomery Street School)

21:15   Signal 9 Station 2227   21:33
         (Green St. and Columbia St.)
         Signal 305 Engine 1

21:20   Truck 6 received a verbal order form Battalion Chief Zoppi to send a man to Engine 14 immediately.

21:25   Signal 9 Station 5452
        (South St. And Hermon St.) (disregard)

21:27   Engine 19 notified by B/C Farley to detail a man to Engine 5.

21:29   Signal 8 Station 3153   21:39
        (7th Ave. & Stone St.)

21:34   Engine 19 contacted Police Radio division for car to transport F/M
        Golombiewski to Engine 5. Car 58 responded as convoy.

21:49   Signal 9 Station 4243   21:59
        (West Runyon St. and Peshine Ave.)

        Truck 10 responded to signal 9 Station 4243 Responded
        to766 Hunterdon Street, 3 story frame. Raised 85' ladder.
        Fire on third floor. Ordered up by B.C. Doll. Out of
        quarters 19 minutes.

21:50   Signal 9 Station 4339   22:27
        (Hawthorne Ave. and Osborne Terr.)
        Signal 300

        Engine 19 received Signal 9 Station
        4339 Osborne and Hawthorne. Responded after pushing
        engine to start it. Ordered up at scene. Returned to
        service on the air and responded to Empire Street. Had
        batteries replaced, returned to quarters. The following
        companies are out of service: Engine 6, 12, 17, 18.

        Engine 6 responded to Hawthorne and Osborne Terrace.
        Signal 300. Engine companies 2, 4, 7, 17, 18 out of
        service.

21:58   Signal 9 Station 2161   22:06
        (James St. and Burnet St.)
        Signal 300

22:12   Signal 8 Station 3443   22:13
        (Berkley Ave. andNorth 3rd St.)   Signal 300

22:14   Signal 9 Station 2413   22:21
        (Emmit St. and Austin St.)   Signal 300

Engine 10 responded to 95 Emmit Street. No cause for alarm.

22:25   Signal 9 Station 4233   23:07
        (Avon Ave. and Bergen St.)

Engine 6 responded to Avon Avenue and Bergen Street. Hooked up feed line to hydrant, stretched two lines 1 ½" pre-connected and one booster. Operated on first and second floors. Pump time thirty minutes. Captain Ryan received nail puncture in left wrist.

22:26   Signal 9 Station 2237
        (East Kinney St. and Orchard St.)

Engine 14 responded to East Kinney and Orchard Streets. Fire at 15 Scott Street, four story, non-fire resistant building. Used one John Bean, one line 2 ½" four lengths, one line 1 ½" two lengths. Three masks @ 30 minutes. Pump time 1 hour thirty minutes. 15 gallons of gas received at this fire from Special Services.

22:29   Engine 14 X manned by Captain D'Augustino, F/M Greeley, Erno, Montalbano, and Wertzel.

22:30   Signal 9, Station 2237   00:25
        (East Kinney St. and Orchard St.)

Truck 1 responded on the above. Used hooks, axes, and ventilated. Out of service 1 hour 55 minutes.

Engine 14 X responded as   00:31
Task Force 2 to 15 Scott Street. Used four lengths 1 ½" on second floor. Engine duty 1 ½ hours. Engines out 6, 10, 11, 12, 18, 20.

22:44   Signal 9, Station 4485   22:51
        (16th Ave and South 14th St.)
22:51   Signal 9, Station 1461   22:54
        (South Orange Ave. and North Munn St.)
        Signal 300

22:56   Signal 9, Station 4151   23:02
(West Runyon St. and Hillside Ave.)

Truck 10 received signal 9 Station 4151. Responded to
Hillside Avenue and West Runyon Street. Raised 24'
ladder at site of previous fire. Ordered up by B.C.
Kinnear.

Engine 10 responded to West Runyon Street. Small fire,
no duty – Engine 29, Signal 308. While returning to
quarters notified by operator to respond to Station 4516.
Auto fire, no duty.

22:57   Signal 9, Station 2237   00:18
(East Kinney St. and Orchard St.)

Truck 3 received signal 9 Station 2237. Responded to
East Kinney and Orchard Streets. Fire in 5 story factory
building. Raised 35' and 25' ladders. Ordered up by
Chief Redden.

Salvage 1 responded to 68 Orchard Street. Used 2 smoke
ejectors. Secured doors on the first floor. At this station
Captain Mahiley (?) fell off the fire escape and was taken
to hospital by Rescue Squad.

23:00   Signal 9, Station 4313
         (15th Ave. and South 8th St.)
         23:01   Signal 9, Station 4244   23:52
                  (West Runyon St. and Badger Ave.)
                  Engine 19 received Station 4244,   23:16
         responded to Badger and West Runyon, redirected on
         radio to rekindle West Runyon and Hillside. Ordered up
         at scene.

23:06   Signal 9, Station 4137   23:46
         (Rose and Monmouth Sts.)

23:10   Signal 9, Station 3257   23:37
         (Mt. Pleasant Ave. and Oriental Pl.)
         Signal 305

Engine 9 responded on a Signal 9 to Station 3227. Found abandoned Ford Fairlane with fire in front seat. Used on booster. No owner or plate available. Car in front of 47 Mt. Pleasant Avenue.

23:11	Signal 9, Station 4516	23:37

(Watson and Ridgewood Aves.)

Truck 10 received a signal 9 Station 4516. Responded to auto fire on Ridgewood Avenue. Overhauled, used hooks and axes. Ordered up by B.C. Kinnear. Trucks out of service 1,2,4,8,9,11.

23:18	Signal 9 Station 2234	23:25

(Washington and West Kinney Sts.)
Engine 10 received and responded to Station 2234, ordered to stretch but did not wet.

23:20	Signal 9 Station 4653	23:32

(Renner and Peshine Aves.)
Engine 19 received signal 9 Station 4653, responded, report of smoke from 41 Renner,   Checked.

23:29	Signal 9, Station 3257	23:42

(Mt. Pleasant Ave. and Oriental Pl.)
Signal 305

23:30	Signal 9 Station 4313	23:40

(15th Ave. and South 8th St.)
Engine 6 responded to 15th Avenue and 8th Street. Molotov cocktail thrown in window of building, 451 15th Avenue. Used booster five minutes.

23:34	Signal 9 Station 4469	23:45

(Schuyler and Irving Aves.)

23:35	Signal 9 Station 1366	23:48

(Cabinet and Camden Sts.)
Truck 3 responded to 350 West Market Street, fire on first floor of 3 story frame building. Ventilated and overhauled. Ordered up by Engine 7.

23:38	Signal 9 Station 4233	23:40

(Avon Ave. and Bergen St.)   Signal 300

23:40   Signal 9 Station 4316   23:46
(16th Ave. and Littleton St.)
Engine 6 responded to 16th and Littleton Avenues. Signal
300. Engine companies 14, 18, 20 Battalion Chief 2 out
of service.

23:51   Signal 5 Engine 12

23:56   Signal 9 Station 2315   00:15
(Chester and Mulberry Sts.)
Engine 10 responded to Chestnut and Mulberry. Signal
305 While out of quarters responded to Mulberry and
Walnut.

24:00   Midnight   *Saturday July 15, 1967*

24:00   Signal 9 Station 4233   00:07
(Avon Ave and Bergen St.)   Signal 300

Engine 6 responded to Avon Avenue and Bergen Street.
Signal 300. Engine companies 1, 12, 14, 18 Battalion
Chiefs 2 and 4 out of service.

00:06   Signal 5 Truck 5   00:51
Tires shot out, changed on Broad Street.

00:10   Signal 9 Station 1337   00:36
(12th Ave. and Camden St.)

Truck 3 received Station 1337. Responded to 45 Camden
Street. Fire on first floor of 2 story frame building. Used
hooks, axes, and masks 20 minutes.

00:12   Signal 9 Station 4143   00:50
(Rose St. and Stratford Pl.)

Truck 10 received Station 4143, signal 9. Responded to
Hillside Place, 3 story frame vacant building, fire on first
and second floors. Raised 85' aerial and 35' ladder. Used
hooks and axes. Out of quarters 43 minutes. Ordered up
by B.C. Greeley.

Engine 10 responded to #31 Hillside Place, fire in 1st and 2nd floor of three story frame dwelling vacant. Used one line 1 ½" three lengths, two lengths 2 ½" for supply from Engine 20. Owner unknown. Engine duty 30 minutes.

00:19   Signal 8 Station 4313   00:30
        (15th Ave. and South 8th St.)
        Engine 6 responded to Signal 9 Station 4313, fire in two story brick factory on south east corner of 15th Avenue and South 8th Street. Pump time 5 minutes. Engine companies 11, 12, 18, 20 out of service.

00:29   Signal 9 Station 2331   00:34
        (Broad St. and Parkhurst St.)   Signal 300

00:36   Signal 5 Engine 12

00:40   Signal 9 Station 1412   00:42
        (Central Ave. and 8th St.)   Signal 300

        00:47   Signal 8 Station 2228   00:47
        *(Mulberry and Walnut Sts.)*Signal 300

01:12   Signal 9 Station 1247   01:12
        (13th Ave. and Wallace St.)   Signal 305

        01:28   Signal 8 Station 1365   01:30
        (12th Ave and Fairmount Ave.)   Signal 300

01:29   Signal 9 Station 3257   01:35
        (Mt. Pleasant Ave. and Oriental St.)   Signal 300

        Engine 9 received and responded to 3257.

01:39   Signal 9 Station 4682   02:27
        (Bergen St. and Hawthorne Pl.)

        Truck 10 responded on signal 9 (booked as 4522 at 10 Truck, others companies books have 4682) to 921 Bergen Street, 3 story frame. Fire on second floor. Raised 35' ladder. Used hooks and axes to ventilate and overhaul. Ordered up by B.C. Doll. Out of quarters 50 minutes.

While working at this fire F/M Werber was struck on right shoulder by debris. Remained on duty.

01:40   Signal 9 Station 2317   01:48
(Pennington St. and Orchard St.)   Signal 305

Engine 14 responded to Pennington and Orchard Streets. Fire located corner of Orchard and Camp Streets. Mattress in street, used 1 booster.

01:44   Signal 9 Station 4337   01:45
(Millington Ave. and Ingrahm Pl.)   Signal 300

       01:52   Signal 5 Engine 6   01:56

Engine 6 responded to rubbish fire in trash at curb in front of 367 Littleton Avenue. Used one booster five minutes. Engine companies 7, 9, 12, 18, 29 out of service.

       01:55   Signal 8 Station 3257   02:00
(Mt. Pleasant Ave. and Oriental St.)   Signal 300

Engine 9 received and responded on Station 3257.

       01:59   Signal 9 Station 4151   02:17
(West Runyon St. and Hillside Ave.)

Engine 10 responded to Hillside and West Runyon. Signal 305, Engine 12.

       02:03   Signal 9 Station 4337   02:07
(Millington Ave. and Ingrahm Pl.)

Engine 6 responded and ordered up enroute. Signal 300. Engine companies 7, 9, 12, 18, 29 out of service.

       02:10   Signal 9 Station 4412   02:15
(Hawthorne Ave. and Clinton Pl.)

Engine 6 responded and ordered up enroute. Signal 300. Engine companies 7, 9, 18, 29 out of service.

02:20   Signal 8 Station 4412   02:22

(Hawthorne Ave. and Clinton Pl.)   Signal 300

02:50   Signal 9 Station 2342   03:10
(Orchard St. and Tichenor St.)

Truck 1 responded to 161 Orchard Street, fire on roof,
used 30-28 ladders, out 20 minutes.

Engine 14 responded to fire located 161 OrchardStreet,
Wright Brothers Food Market roof. Cause 2 Molotov
Cocktails. Used 1 John Bean pump 5 minutes.

03:01   Signal 5 Truck 7   03:44

03:12   Signal 9 Station 3241   03:20
(Chester Ave. and Hinsdale Pl.)   Signal 300

03:20   Unidentified woman to Engine 10's quarters to inform
company that a woman at 15 Astor Street was to deliver a baby.
Notified Radio Police.

03:20   Signal 9 Station 4117   04:43
(Morton St and Prince St.)
Engine 6 responded to a working fire at 95 Prince Street,
three story vacant building. Stretched eight lengths 2 ½"
to hydrant on corner of Morton and Pince. Stretched one
line four lengths 1 ½" hose. Pump time eighty minutes.
All Engine companies available.

04:09   Station 4214   04:12
(Springfield Ave and Sayre St.) Signal 300

05:27   Signal 9 Station 2317   05:40
(Pennington and Orchard Sts.)   Signal 305

Engine 14 responded. Rubbish fire Elder Place used one
booster.

05:32   Signal 5 Engine 14   05:35
05:40   Signal 9 Station 3255   05:45
(Broad St. and Harvey St.) Signal 305 Eng 9

06:14   Signal 9 Station 4117   08:04

(Morton and Prince Sts.)   Signal 305

Engine 6 responded to fire in a four story brick. Raised extension ladder, used 2 boosters. Pump time eighty minutes. One hundred ten minutes company time.

06:25   Signal 9 Station 5442   06:38
(Delancy and Stockton Sts.)   Signal 305
Engine 27 responded to 118 Stockton Street, Pump Restaurant, compressor motor fire, used booster.

07:17   Engine 14 – B.C. Greeley's orders. One officer and four men to be on duty from 0800. Men are to be supplied by tour 1 and 3 if needed.

07:57   Signal 9 Station 4117   08:30
(Morton and Prince Sts.)
08:00   Tour 1   *Saturday July 15, 1967*

Fireman Joseph Lord of Engine 10 woke up this morning in quarters with a badly swollen and aching left knee. At Station 4151 yesterday afternoon at 14:17 a heavy grate fell on his knee.

11:05   Signal 5 Engine 1   12:32

11:10   Signal 9 Station 4143   11:13
(Rose St. and Stratford Pl.)   Signal 300

        12:05   Signal 9 Station 2871   12:36
        (Kretchmer Homes, 344 Dayton St.)
        Signal 305

        Engine 19 responded on a signal 9 to Station 2871.
        Found clogged incinerator between fourth and fifth floors.
        Used 1 length 1 ½" hose from standpipe on fifth floor to
        clear incinerator 344 Dayton
        Street.

12:23   Signal 5 Engine 16   12:32

        13:30   Engine 10 Register 109 back from Prospect Street, city carpenters installed plywood roof over the cab of register 109 for protection of personnel.

13:51   Signal 9 Station 4117   14:43
(Morton and Prince Sts.)
Engine 6 responded to 83 Prince Street, small fire third
floor. Signal 305 Engine 20. Ordered to stand by for
assistance by Battalion Chief 4. Company time fifty-two
minutes.

14:00   Signal 9 Station 2317   14:08
(Pennsylvania Ave. and Orchard St.) Signal 305

Engine 14 responded to looted tavern at 32 Pennington
Street. Fire in door. Used booster and axes. Engine duty
5 minutes.

Engine 10 responded, reported shooting in the area.

14:25   Signal 9 Station 1148   14:38
(Central Ave. and Lock St.)   Signal 305

14:40   Special Services in Engine 14's quarters. Removed spare
apparatus #45 to Engine 13.

14:45   **Notified by Chief Redden through D.C. Kelly and B.C. Reheis
that roll call will be 1 officer and 6 men trucks, 1 officer and 5
men Engines, and 2 officers and 8 men in 2 piece companies,
no acting officers.**

15:00   Engine 19 notified by B.C. Schick that at 6 P.M. the roll shall be 1
officer, 5 men on duty. One man detailed from Tour 1. The
remaining 3 men on Tour 1 are to report to Engine 2 and man
Register 42.

15:45   Engine 14 received telephone order from B.C. Schmidt that three
men from tour 1 will stay tonight (7/15) and ride with tour 3.
Firemen D'Ambrosio, Gaynor, and Radecke. Captain Linhoff is
detailed to Truck 4 for the night.

15:47   Signal 9 Station 3131   16:14
(7ᵗʰ Ave. opposite Wood St.)   Signal 308

15:55   Truck 6 Captain Sochan notified Newark Police at the request of a
citizen that window smashing and looting of property at Broadway
and Oriental.

16:04   Signal 9 Station 3845   16:14
        (Columbus Homes, 14 Sheffield Dr.) Signal 305

16:16   Signal 9 Station 4161   16:25
        (Rose and Barclay Sts.)   Signal 305

        Engine 10 responded to Rose and Barclay. Auto fire, Engine 12.

        16:30   Signal 9 Station 2212   17:19
        (Broad St. and Edison Pl.)   Signal 305

17:07   Signal 9, Station 2316   17:18
        (McCarter Hwy. and Pennington St.)
        Signal 305

        Engine 14 notified by operator to respond. Found Molotov Cocktail burning on roof of one story cinder block building at 117 Pennington Street. Used booster, 24' ladder, and axe to strip tar paper. Engine duty 5 minutes.

        By order of Battalion Chief P.A. Smith Truck 6 will ride with 1 officer and 6 men tonight 7/15/67. The above entry by Captain Sochan.

17:21   Signal 8, Station 3513   17:50
        (Mt. Pleasant Ave. and Heller Pkwy.)
        Found no fire at 735 Mt. Prospect Ave.

17:43   Signal 9, Station 4117   17:52
        (Morton and Prince Sts.)
        Engine 6 responded and ordered up upon arrival. Signal 308. Engine company 20 out of service.

18:00   Tour 3   *Saturday July 15, 1967*

        Truck 6 has 1 officer and 3 men with 3 additional men from the first tour. (Captain from the first tour standing by.) Engine 19: Engine 20 and Truck 1 out.

        18:15   Signal 9, Station 4131   18:20

(Spruce St. and Barclay St.)   Signal 305

Engine 10 responded to 158 Barclay Street. Signal 305
for Engine 12.

18:21   Signal 9, Station 4572   18:30
        (Aldine St. and Edmond Pl.)
        18:25   Signal 5 Engine 6   20:30

Engine company 6 out of service due to exchange of
gunfire in front of quarters between snipers in Hayes
Project and State Police, City Police, and National Guard.

        18:31   Signal 5 Battalion 4   20:32

        Sniper.

        18:42   Signal 9, Station 4236   18:55
        (Clinton and Badger Aves.) Signal 300

18:55   **Rec'd Signal 9- 9 The curtailment signal was sounded. By
        order of Chief Redden all alarms sounded will respond with 2
        engines, 1 truck and 1 Battalion Chief (and Salvage) until
        further notice.**

19:00   Captain Schwiestzer reported in quarters with spare
        register 40, F/M Giovenco, F/M Mullen, and F/M Mizia.
        Called mechanic on condition of apparatus, also called
        D.C. Dolak about no masks available on apparatus.

19:21   Station 1487   19:22
        (Central Ave. and 9th St.)   Signal 300

19:39   Station 2237   19:47
        (East Kinney St. and Orchard St.)   Signal 305 Engine 1
20:14   B.C. Greeley entered quarters, complied with G.O. 231. Supplied
        Engine 14 X with
        2 masks by orders of Chief Greeley.

20:16   Station 4117   20:32
        (Morton and Prince Sts.)
20:36   Station 4161   20:38
        (Rose and Barclay Sts.)   Signal 300

20:56   Station 4728   21:10
(Scudder Homes, Morton and Lincoln Sts.)
Engine 6 responded and ordered up upon arrival. Signal
308.

21:03   Station 3212   21:09
(Summer Ave. and Kearny St.)   Signal 305

21:10   Station 4329   21:13
(Madison and Seymour Aves.)   Signal 300

        21:13   Station 4334   21:18
                    (Madison Ave. and Seymour Aves.)   Signal 300

        21:35   Signal 5 Engine 2   21:55

        21:48   Station 3131   21:52
                    (7th Ave. opposite Wood St.)   Signal 305

21:51   Station 3244   22:07
(Delavan Ave. and Oraton St.)

Truck 6 responded to truck burning on Oraton Street with
a Molotov cocktail burning on the sidewalk near a
building.

21:57   **5-5-5 Attention buildings in the Scudder Homes have no
elevators working. No water on the upper floors. Companies
hook up on the first floor.**

22:00   Station 5137
(Ferry St. and Lexington St.)

22:03   Station 1437
(13th Ave. and 8th St.)

22:10   Station 4313   22:22
(15th Ave. and 8th St.)

Engine 6 responded to two story brick factory on south
east corner of 15th Avenue and 8th Street. Molotov

cocktail thrown through window. Used one booster five minutes. Engine companies 7, 11 out of service.

22:14   **Station 6155**   00:30
(500 Central Ave. between South 7th and South 8th Sts.)

22:42   Station 5422   23:00
(Chestnut and Pacific Sts.)   Signal 305
Engine 14 responded to Pacific and Orchard Street. Molotov Cocktail, another on Oliver Street near McWhorter Street. Used John Bean pump 3 minutes.

22:44   Station 4243
(West Runyon St. and Peshine Ave.)
Truck 10 received Station 4243. Responded to 312 Peshine Avenue, 3 story frame, fire on second floor. Forced entry, raised 35' ladder, 20' ladder, overhauled. Out of quarters 17 minutes.

22:45   Station 1631   22:50
(Ivy St. and Chapman St.)   Signal 300

22:45   ***Governor's Commission reports Captain Moran killed.***
         22:50   Station 5477   23:15
        (Chestnut and Pacific Sts.)   Signal 308

Engine 14 responded to a truck fire.

23:02   Station 3273   23:15
(Broadway and Delavan Ave.)   Signal 305

23:08   Station 4136   23:15
(Waverly Ave. and Somerset St.)   Signal 305
Engine 10 responded to Waverly and Barclay. Signal 305 Engine 12.

23:15   **Orders of Headquarters 1A – When responding to an alarm of fire and gun fire is in the area, all companies are not to enter the gun fire area – Director Caufield.**

23:19   Station 3257
(Mt. Pleasant Ave. and Oriental St.)   Signal 305

23:29   Station 5128   23:29
(Ferry St. and Niagara St.)   Signal 300

       23:55   Station 4453   00:05
       (South 12th St. and Rawley St., South of 16th Ave.)

Engine 6 responded and ordered up upon arrival. Signal
300. Engine 11 out of service.

24:00   Midnight   *Sunday July 16, 1967*

00:02   Station 4162
(Avon Ave. and Hillside Ave.)   Signal 300

       00:14   Signal 5 Engine 12   07:50

                Gunfire.

       00:15   Signal 5 Truck 5   07:50

       Gunfire.

00:16   Station 1349   00:55
(South Orange Ave. and Camden St.)
Engine 6 responded to fire at 210 Camden Street. Used
one booster 25 minutes. Engine companies 4, 9, 11, 12,
13 Battalion Chief 3 out of service.

00:35   **Received radio message. Keep clear of Bergen Street and
Clinton Avenue. Heavy gunfire at this location.**

00:50   Station 3273   02:45
(Broadway and Delavan Ave.)
Truck 6 responded to a fire in a vacant building on
Delavan Place. Stretched 2 ½ and overhauled.

Salvage 1 responded to a small fire.   01:30

**01:30 Miscellaneous – Salvage 1 transported
National Guard all over the city, between 01:30 and
07:07.**

00:51   Station 3423   01:20
(Park Ave. and North 13th St.)

00:55   Station 3273   02:13
         (Broadway and Delavan Ave.)
         (Task Force #2)

         01:00   Signal 5 Engine 10   07:10

Engine 10 put on a Signal 5 due to gunfire outside of
firehouse both front and back. National Guardsmen on
duty returning fire.

01:05   **On orders of Chief Redden all companies responding on an
alarm are not to use sirens, bells, or red lights. Proceed with
caution.**

01:53   **Radio message – all Battalion Chiefs to report to armory
(Roseville) at 02:30.**

01:55   **Do not respond on Belmont Avenue. Heavy gunfire.**

02:20   Station 6461   03:30
         (42 Garden St. between N.J.R.R. Ave. and McWhorter St.)

Truck 1 responded to 42 Garden Street. Replaced three
sprinkler heads, used 14' ladder. Out 1 hour 10 minutes.

Engine 14 responded to 42 Garden Street. Fire in one
story brick on East Kinney Street. Used one John Bean
pump 20 Minutes.

03:05   **Two National Guardsmen in Truck 6's quarters assigned to
Engine 13 and
            will ride on apparatus.**

03:10   Battalion Chief Farley in Engine 19's
    quarters, left orders that 2 National Guardsmen are to
ride with us. Guardsmen Frank Pannelli and Ronnie Alea
reported in quarters for duty.

03:29   Station 1436   03:43
         (12th Ave. and 11th Street)
03:30   Out: Engine 10 (return 08:12), 11 (08:12), 12 (07:47), Trucks 5, 11
    (08:12)

03:33   **Sig 5-5-5 by order of Chief Redden, all units on all alarms sounded. The Batt. Chief will respond only. No companies will respond until requested by chief of that district. Effective immediately, until further notice.**

04:30   Engine 10 left quarters after all Guradsmen and Police left. Pumper and Tour 1 to Engine 19's quarters. Wagon and Tour 3 to Engine 1's quarters. Returned at 09:00 Sunday July 16 and found everything intact (OK). Also found 16 Guardsmen. Company riding two guardsmen on each piece. Notified operator company in service at 09:00.

04:35   Engine 10 unit #2 in Engine 19 quarters on detail.

05:45   Truck 10

           On orders of Chief Redden through Chief McCormack the regular roll call for the 1st Tour tomorrow will be followed.

07:07   Station 1343   07:23
           (South Orange Ave. and Bergen St.)

           Truck 3 received Station 1343. Responded, fire in basement of two story frame at 190 Bergen Street, used hooks and ventilated.
           Engine 6 responded to fire in rags in cellar of 210 Bergen Street. Two and a half story frame tenement. Owner unknown. Used one booster, five minutes. Engine companies 10, 11, 12 out of service.

07:47   Station 4122   07:51
           (Court and Broome Sts.)   Signal 305

08:00   **Tour 1** *Sunday July 16, 1967*

           Truck 6 riding 1 & 3. Truck 1 riding 1 & 4. Engine 14 riding 1 & 4. Truck 4 riding 0 & 4.

           At 0800 Captain Sochan of Truck 6 reported for duty found 2 Military Guards at company quarters armed and responding to alarms with this company. PFC Geo. W. McCabe and Geo. Davis SP4 from Co. B 2nd Battalion "M" 114 Infantry. They reported to quarters at 0300 on 7/16/67 Riots in progress City of Newark, New Jersey.

10:05   Station 1229   10:15
(Hudson and Hartford Sts.)

Truck 3 Received Station 1229, vacant building, reported extinguished by a civilian.

10:13   **Received verbal message from Director Caufield when companies responding
to or working at a fire are fired upon the order is to "GET OUT"**

10:29   **By order of Chief Redden. All companies responding to alarms or at the scene of a fire, if fired upon, withdraw from the scene immediately.**

10:33   **B.C. Smith in quarters, order flag to be flown at half mast.**

12:00   Station 4513   12:06
(Meeker and Hillside Aves.)   Signal 300

Engine 19 received Station 4513, BC 4 reported Signal 300.

        13:00   Signal 5 Engine 20   13:17

        13:01   Signal 5 Truck 5   13:14

13:02   Signal 5 Battalion 4   13:16

        13:08   Station 1442   13:16
        (South Orange Ave. and 12th St.)
13:03   Whereas the National Guard left Engine 10's quarters and that a woman was shot in front of quarters (about 10:50) and company had no protection, company left quarters to Engine 19's quarters. Returned under armed guard at 14:01. Same armed guard (National Guardsman) returned to Engine 19 at 14:02.

13:09   Engine 10 unit #1 and unit #2 to ride out of Engine 19 quarters.

13:31   Station 3263   13:51
(Mt. Pleasant Ave. and Clark St.)

B.C. Smith ordered a signal 9. Truck 6 responded as additional help and responded with 2 State Police cars.

13:59 **5-5-5 Received verbal order that the following schedule for the next 4 nights will be worked by all units Sunday Tour 2 with Tour # 4 – Monday Tour 1 – with Tour 4 – Tuesday Tour 4 with Tour #1 – Wednesday Tour 3 – with Tour #1 – Note – the above are only nights. The above order by Chief Engineer J. Redden**

14:29   Station 4211   15:00
         (15th Ave. and Bruce St.)
         Truck 3 Received and responded to Station 4211, 15th Avenue. 4 story brick vacant. Ventilated and overhauled.

         Engine 6 responded to 328 15th Avenue, four story brick. Fire on second and third floor, used one 1 ½" and one booster. Engine duty thirty minutes. Company time fifty minutes. Owner unknown.

15:17 **5-5-5 The following will be the roll call on companies at night, Truck Cos. 1 & 6, Rescue and Salvage 1 & 5, two piece companies 2 & 8, one piece companies 1 & 5. Spares 1 & 4 By order of Chief Redden.**

15:40   Station 1415   16:08
             (Sussex Ave. and Myrtle Ave.)

15:42   Station 3244   15:50
         (Devalan Ave. and Oraton St.)   Signal 305 Eng 13

             16:59   Signal 5 Engine 26   17:07

17:05   Station 4427   17:09
         (Madison Ave. and South 14th St.) Signal 300

17:43   Station 4233
         (Avon Ave. and Bergen St.)   Signal 300

17:49 **Received 4- 4-4-4 Re: Announce with deep regret the death of Captain Michael Moran.**

18:00 **Tour 4 and Tour 2   *Sunday July 16, 1967***

Truck 10, 1 officer & 6 men Truck 1, 1 officer & 6 men .
Truck 4, 1 officer & 6 men.

Engine 14 tour 4 and members of tour 2, 1 & 5, members
of the NJ National Guard detailed to ride with company.
SP John Stuffo & SP Joe Reed.

Engine 10 Tour 4 has no Police or Guard protection.

18:25   Engine 10 notified Radio Police of a man and woman lying on
corner of Sherman and Murray bleeding.

18:40   Two National Guardsmen reported in quarters, four more
Guardsmen reported in.

19:00   Station 3846   19:09
(Columbus Homes, 7th Ave. and Sheffield Dr.)

Salvage 1 stood by in quarters, ordered to return by
Battalion 3.

        19:14   Signal 5 Engine 9   19:15

19:15   Engine 10 now riding split unit 1 and unit 2. Unit 1 is the Fourth
Tour riding 1 officer and 4 men. Unit 2 is the Second Tour riding
1 officer and 4 men. Captain Seavey Unit 1 and Captain Caldwell
Unit 2.

19:17   Station 4241   19:20 *(West Bigelow*
        St. and Hunterdon St.) Signal 300

19:26   Station 4118   19:29
        (Montgomery and Prince Sts.)
20:10   Station 5216   20:13
        (New Jersey Railroad Ave. and Elm St.) Signal 300

Salvage 1 responded and ordered to quarters by BC 5.

20:11   Station 4186   20:18
        (Mercer and Howard Sts.) Signal 300

20:10   One firefighter from tour 2 reported for duty at Truck 6.

20:15   Engine 6 administered first aid to Pasquale Copoliano, age eighty, of 424 South 9th Street for head wound caused by bottle thrown by person unknown on 15th Avenue. Victim removed to City Hospital by National Guard.

20:50   Captain March reported for duty at Truck 6.

20:55   Station 3224   20:59
              (Broad St. and 3rd Ave.)
              Fire bomb, out on arrival. Salvage 1 stood by in quarters.

21:01   Station 4132   21:07
              (Spruce and Monmouth Sts.)   Signal 305

21:19 – 23:14   Additional members reported to Engine 14 to man 14 X.

21:20   Station 1421   21:24
              (West Market and Gray Sts.)   Signal 300

21:38   Station 4118   21:55
              (Montgomery and Prince Sts.)

21:54   Station 2228   21:58
              (Mulberry and Walnut Sts.)   Signal 305

              Salvage 1 responded on stand by in quarters.

22:36   Station 5253   22:40
              (Lafayette and McWhorter Sts.)   Signal 305

                     Salvage 1 stand by in quarters.

22:48   Station 3467   Task Force #1   23:47
              (Berkley Ave. and 5th St.)

              Salvage 1 responded to 860 No. 5th Street, fire on second floor, removed water, secured building, used 30' paper.

22:51   Station 4598   22:58
              (Chadwick Ave. and Jeffrey Place)   Signal 300

23:14   Station 4243   23:22
              (West Runyon St. and Peshine Ave.)   Signal 305

24:00 **Midnight** *Monday July 17, 1967*

00:15 Station 1249   00:19
(South Orange Ave and Hunterdon St.)
Signal 300

00:15 Signal 5 Engine 6   00:26

Engine 6 our of service because of sniper fire.

00:30   Signal 5 Battalion 4   01:00

00:35   Station 3137   01:10
(6*th* Ave. and Cutler St.)   Signal 300

01:24 Station 4169   02:00
(Spruce and Prince Streets)

Engine 6 responded to Spruce and Prince Streets.
Assisted Engine 12 with lines in abandoned building.

03:02 Station 4244
(West Runyon St. and Badger Ave.)
Signal 300

07:45 Additional members manning Engine 14 X left quarters.

08:00 **Tour 2** *Monday July 17, 1967*

(Truck 6 - 1 officer & 3 men. Truck 1 – 1 officer & 3 men) PFC
George W. McCabe & George Davis SP4 are riding with Truck 6
apparatus with arms for protection.

08:33   Station 5193   08:44
(Blanchard St. at the Passaic River)

08:55 **Rec'd Sig 5 – 5 – 5 Curtailment order 2 – ENGINES & 1
TRUCK & 1 BC shall ride on all alarms**

08:59   Signal 5 Truck 5   14:26

09:04 Signal 5 Engine 32

09:17   **Rec'd Sig 5 – 5 – 5 all in service inspections & training academy classes discontinued until further notice.**

09:40   **Rec'd Sig 5 – 5 – 5 Clarification: 2 ENG & 1 TRUCK & 1 BC shall ride on all alarms until 6 PM**

09:54   Station 4323   09:59
(South 10th St. and Blum St.)

Engine 6 received and responded to Station 4323. Auto fire in front of 19 Gold Street. 1966 Cadallaris convertible, license #HHP 637, serial # 17061 white. Owner Ralph Sanks, Jr. 500 South 19th Street, carburetor. Out on arrival.

10:17   Signal 5 Engine 1   11:36

10:17   Station 2518   10:22
(Frelinghuysen Ave. and Whittier Pl.)
Signal 305

Engine 19 received Station 2518 – 727 Frelinghuysen Avenue. Passing light smoke condition caused by cutting bakelite with electric saw. Citizen saw smoke coming out of vent.

10:22   Test signal over the desk bell

10:45   Signal 5 Engine 1   11:37
11:42   Signal 5 Engine 6   11:53

Notified by citizen of gas leak at four story brick at 309 Springfield Avenue. Responded on a Signal 5 and shut off all gas in the building. Notified the operator to have Public Service respond.

12:36   Signal 5 Engine 29   12:46

13:30   F/M Joe Muller of Truck 4 left quarters, detailed to Burns Funeral Home.

14:02   Signal 5 Engine 27   14:31

Responded on signal 5 to U.S. Route 1, gasoline spill, used one booster line 15 minutes. Out of quarters 25 minutes.

14:07   Citizen Mary from 322 Hunterdon   14:09
Street in quarters, requested radio car to take her to City Hospital. She is in labor.

15:14   Station 4434   Task Force #1   15:57
(Avon Ave. and South 15th St.)
15:16   Station 4434   Task Force #2   15:33

Engine 6 received and responded on 2nd task force on Signal 9 to Station 4434 to a three story frame at 786 Avon Avenue. Assisted Engine 18. Ordered up by Deputy Chief Marsh.

15:20   Station 3257   15:30
(Mt. Pleasant Ave. and Oriental St.)

Truck 6 responded to a signal 300, ordered up by B.C. 3

15:25   **B.C. Zieser and two military trucks at Engine 14's quarters and took SP 4 Stuffo & Reed aboard.**

15:57   **National Guard left Engine 19's quarters.**

16:03   **PFC Geo W. McCabe & Geo. Davis SP4 left quarters.**
16:06   Signal 5 Engine 18   16:08

16:30   **Rec'd 5 – 5 – 5 – all off duty men Rosary prays for Captain Moran Tues 8 PM at Burns Funeral Home.**

16:35   Station 1323   17:30
(Orange and 3rd Sts.)

16:37   Signal 5 Engine 19   16:49

Engine 19 notified by operator to respond to 500 Frelinghuysen Avenue, see office manager. Switchboard operator received phone call of bomb planted in factory. Called operator to notify police, ordered to return to quarters.
16:45   Station 4264   18:56

(Clinton Pl. and Peshine Ave.)
16:54   Signal 10 Station 4264 Task Force #2   18:57

Engine 6 received and responded on 2nd task force Signal 9 Station 4264 to fire involving clothing store at 454 Clinton Avenue, one story non-fire resistant. Stretched one line 1 ½" four lengths to protect exposure on left. Stretched one line 2 ½" three lengths to Engine 18 for feed. Engine duty thirty minutes. Used four masks five minutes each.

16:55   **Notice #77 Death of Captain Moran
Funeral Wednesday 09:00 at Truck 12.**

17:00   Salvage 1 – F/M Nardone, Whalen, Florio, and Captain Hestor reported for duty. Notified they were not wanted.

18:00   **Tours 4 and 1   *Monday July 17, 1967***
(Truck 6 -1 officer & 6 men. Truck 1 – 1 officer & 6 men.)

18:25   **Recd signal 5 – 5 - - 5 . By order of Director Caufield in the event of any shooting at any alarm response apparatus shall leave that location.**

18:30   **To all off duty. All those who would like to say the rosary for the repose of the soul of the late Captain Michael Moran shall report to the Burns Funeral Home, 462 Sanford Ave Newark Tuesday July 18, 1967 at 8 PM**

Four Newark policemen from car #131 in Engine 10's quarters to remain all night.

19:12   Signal 5 Engine 20   19:32

19:16   Battalion Chief Wall delivered Notice #77 pertaining to the funeral of Captain
Moran of Engine 11 to Engine 6.

20:15   Station 1443   20:36
(South Orange Ave. and 14th St.)

Engine 6 responded to Station 1443. Ordered up at scene, Signal 308.

20:45   Five Patrolmen in Engine 6's quarters to ride with company, one to ride with Chief.

21:35   Station 2144   22:30
        (McCarter Hwy. and Centre St.)
        Truck 1 responded, fire foot of Center Street, raised 85'Snorkel, 25' ladder, ventilated one hole. Our 50 minutes.

        Salvage 1 responded to 164 Centre Street, Hillside Trading Company. Assisted companies, first aid given to James Poetpowell, slight burn on right arm.

21:35   Station 4227   21:58
        (Bergen St. & Waverly Ave.)

        Engine 6 received and responded to Station 4227. Ordered up, Signal 305

21:45   Station 4611   21:54
        (Watson & Jelliff Aves.)
        Engine 19 received Station 4611. Signal 300 by Deputy Chief 1.

22:00   Station 4343   22:23
        (Clinton & Chadwick Aves.)

22:35   Station 3244   22:39
        (Delavan Ave. and Oraton St.

        Received Station 3244, Signal 300. Out 5 minutes.

        Salvage 1 responded on stand by in quarters.

        22:36   Signal 5 Engine 6   22:46

        Engine 6 responded to 49 Bedford Street. Auto seat burning in street. Used one booster five minutes.

24:00 Midnight   *Tuesday July 18, 1967*

00:10   Station 1343   01:16

(South Orange Ave. and Bergen St.)

Truck 3 responded to 214 Camden Street. Found furniture warehouse on fire, used hooks and axes force entry and overhauled, used 14' baby ladder. Out of quarters 66 minutes. F/M DeMarzo received small cut on left hand.

Engine 6 responded to 210 Camden Street, three story brick. Owner Paul Metnik, Princeton Road, Cranford, NJ. Fire involved furniture store on first floor. Stretched and operated two lines of pre-connected 1 ½" four lengths each to first floor. Pump time fifty minutes.

01:12   Station 4458   01:21
            (16th Ave. and 16th St.)

Engine 6 responded to a Signal 300.

02:54   Station 5445   04:35
            (Pacific and East Kinney Streets)

Truck 1 responded to 249 East Kinney Street, three story frame. Used 35', 30', 24', 16' ladders, hooks, axes, ventilated, and overhauled.

Engine 14 responded to 249-251 East Kinney Street. 2 ½ story attached frames, fire in attic. Used two lines 1 ½", four lengths each, took feed from Engine 5. Masks 4 @ 30 minutes, engine duty 1 ½ hours. All units in service.

Salvage 1 responded to 251 East Kinney Street, assisted companies,Used smoke ejector and generator.

04:00   Patrolmen relieved by five other patrolmen
 at Engine 6's quarters, one riding with gig.

06:58   Signal 5 Engine 29   07:06

07:00   Patrolmen left Engine 6's quarters.

07:24   Station 4455   08:50

(16th Ave. and 13th St.)

Received and responded to Station 4455 on first task
force to a fire involving third floor rear three story frame
at 561 South 12th Street. Stretched one line 2 ½" five
lengths from hydrant as feed. Stretched one line 1 ½"
four lengths to third floor and operated on same and
cockloft. Used five masks ten minutes each. Engine duty
eighty minutes. Tour 2 relieved Tour 4 at fire. Owner M.
Miller, 11 North 6th
Street. Tenant third floor left Anne Seward, third floor
right, Josephine Reese. A second task force was called.

07:30   Station 4455   Task Force 2   08:11

07:49   Engine 9 notified via telephone that F/M Connelly has
been informed to report to his National Guard unit immediately.

07:50   Station 3239   08:38
         (Broadway and Chester Avenue)

Engine 9 responded on a Signal 9 Station 3239 to 512
Broadway, 2 ½ story frame. Small fire third floor, used 1
line 1 ½" three lengths. Pumped low pressure hydrant in
front of 489 Broadway. Stretched six lengths 2 ½" feed
for wagon. Pump duty Register 43 twenty minutes,
register 65 twenty minutes, total forty minutes. Used
three masks five minutes each. Out 1 hour.

Truck 6 responded to 512 Broadway, found a mattress on
third floor burning. Company ordered to ventilate third
floor and roof. Laddered building 25' to second floor
roof and 100' aerial to attic roof. 3 masks 5 minutes each.
Signal 308.

08:00   **Tour 2   *Tuesday July 18***

Wednesday July 19

09:23   B.C. Greeley visited Engine 14. Gave verbal orders of response to
box alarms. First due company only until notified differently.

09:41   Accident report from Captain Caldwell and R. Suchodakshi taken.

11:00   Trucks 1 officer & 5 men at night, Battalion Chief response at night remains the same.

18:00   Officer Edward O'Neill NPD arrived in quarters to ride with Battalion 3 as armed guard.

Thursday July 20

A Police officer is still riding with Battalion 5.

12:14   Fireman James Murtash of Special Service picked up the following articles of
clothing belonging to deceased Captain Moran: one rubber coat, one pair black pants, one pair boots, one pair gloves, one pair socks, one pair shorts. No shirt, undershirt, or helmet.

Police still riding with Engine 6 at night.

Saturday July 22

19:20   Engine 19 notified by Second Battalion Chief Leonard that company is to roll on boxes in presumed non-critical areas

19:25   Engine 19 called Battalion Chief 4 McCormack to check on procedure in the Fourth Battalion. Instructed to remain in quarters until called unless fire can be observed from quarters in which case company is to roll in.

19:30   Four Newark policemen and car #119 arrive at Engine 10's quarters to ride with them. Police ride nights with Engine 10 until end of July 23/24 night tour.

Sunday July 23

07:00   Beginning 08:00 hours the Newark Fire
Department will resume normal running operations.

Last night police ride with Engine 6.

Monday July 24

Police ride with Battalion Chief 3 until 0800.

Wednesday July 26

Engine 9: Notice # 80 regarding overtime delivered.

Thursday July 27

18:00   Engine 9: Reduced assignment in effect (a signal 8-8 was transmitted) two engines, one truck, and a Battalion Chief on each alarm. If more help is needed call for task force.

Friday July 28

14:15   Engine 19: 5-5-5-5 Response to fires on a box alarm two engine companies, one truck company, a Battalion Chief, and Salvage will respond. If second task force is needed two engines, one truck, and the Deputy Chief will respond. On third task force a Battalion Chief will also respond with two engines, one truck.

Monday July 31

Battalion Chief left an envelope in 19 Engine's quarters for contributions to fund for Captain Moran and Detective Toto.

Thursday August 3

Chief Tauriello informed Engine 19 that Register 32 hose wagon should be ready from body shop
Saturday August 5 about noon.

Saturday August 5

Register 32 hose wagon will be ready about noon Monday August 7.

Monday August 14

Engine 19 picked up Register 32 from body shop, found rear window in cab broken during riots.

Thursday August 24

105

15:23   Engine 19's book: Special blood bank class for Michael Moran, family on August 29, 15:00 – 19:00 at Academy.

Tuesday September 19

Memorial Mass for Captain Moran and Detective Toto at Scared Heart Church.

www.ingramcontent.com/pod-product-compliance
Lightning Source LLC
Chambersburg PA
CBHW051814040426
42446CB00007B/673